ON PALESTINE

On Palestine

Noam Chomsky
and Ilan Pappé

Edited by Frank Barat

Haymarket Books
Chicago, Illinois

© 2015 Frank Barat, Noam Chomsky, and Ilan Pappé

Haymarket Books
P.O. Box 180165
Chicago, IL 60618
773-583-7884
info@haymarketbooks.org
www.haymarketbooks.org

ISBN: 978-1-60846-470-8

Trade distribution:
In the US, Consortium Book Sales and Distribution, www.cbsd.com
In the UK, Turnaround Publisher Services, www.turnaround-uk.com
In Canada, Publishers Group Canada, www.pgcbooks.ca
All other countries, Ingram Publisher Services International,
IPS_Intlsales@ingramcontent.com

Cover design by Christine Knowlton.

This book was published with the generous support of Lannan
Foundation and the Wallace Action Fund.

Printed in the United States.

Entered into digital printing September 2018.

Library of Congress Cataloging in Publication data is available.

Contents

INTRODUCTION

How did you become an activist? Why Palestine?

These are the types of questions many activists will be asked at one point or another when talking about their life, work, and motivations with a "non-activist" person. While I often want to reverse the question and ask, "Why *aren't* you an activist?," I usually decide, with insight, to try my best in answering this potentially frustrating question.

Why? Because I think it is important to understand where the questions are coming from, and it is as important to look inside yourself, take a step back, relive your journey, pause, and realize that you too, not that long ago, may have asked the same questions of anyone engaged in working toward a better world—where equality, justice, and freedom apply to all, regardless of nationality, ethnicity, country of origin, skin color, political affiliation, or sexual orientation.

How, then, does one become an activist?

The easy answer would be to say that we do not become activists; we simply forget that we are. We are all born with compassion, generosity, and love for others inside us. We are all moved by injustice and discrimination. We are all, inside, concerned human beings. We all want to give more than to receive. We all want to live in a world where solidarity and companionship are more important values than individualism and selfishness. We all want to share beautiful things; experience joy, laughter, love; and experiment, together.

But we have a problem. A big one. We live in a society, and an epoch, where we do not have time to think any longer. We live in a time when taking a step back and a deep breath have become a luxury that many cannot afford.

We live in a world where the mainstream education system teaches you to obey and listen to authority from the earliest age and does not offer you the chance to think for yourself and express yourself in ways that are outside the proclaimed norm.

We live in a society where the "nothing" (shopping, watching TV) has become a "something" and the "something" (relaxing, meditating, sharing) has become a void in need of being filled. Our minds, our souls, have slowly been corrupted by materialistic nothingness that has been created for us, billboarded in front of our eyes, and printed, tattooed on our cells by advertising, marketing, and vulture capitalism.

The "remote control" of our world only has two buttons, "Play" and "Fast Forward," while the one we are all looking for is the "Pause."

I "became" an activist through books.

After having worked since my early twenties in various menial jobs, and like a good citizen doing my nine to five, looking away at the ticking clock, enjoying my life for the reasons I was told were needed to enjoy it, fulfilling the potential that I had been "allowed" to have by society and its "leaders," I stopped.

I quit my job, moved from the city I had been living in for the last six years, and started studying again. I read loads of books and realized that I wanted this period, which was supposed to be temporary (because of the dread of unemployment and boredom potentially creeping in), to last forever.

Reading and feeling enlightened by those books really played a big part in changing my vision of life and what it was supposed to mean. I started with reading Chomsky and slowly became very interested in anything that had to do with Israel/Palestine. Reading Edward Said, Mahmoud Darwish, Ghassan Kanafani, John Berger, Tanya Reinhart, Ilan Pappé, Norman Finkelstein, Noam Chomsky, Kurt Vonnegut, Arundhati Roy, Naomi Klein . . . all became part of my daily routine.

Books changed me and I think that they are, more than anything else, one of the best tools we can use to learn, reflect on, and truly understand the world we are living in. They are a bridge between languages, continents, and people. A book will accompany you and will stay with you, it will mark you like nothing else. You will go back to it, quote it, argue about it. You will borrow one and lend one. The written word, in my opinion, is therefore more effective and long lasting than the spoken one as a tool for change.

I felt very lucky and privileged, when, in 2008, two of the authors I had read again and again on Palestine, Professors Noam Chomsky and Ilan Pappé, agreed to work on a book with me. Our long email exchanges became *Gaza in Crisis: Reflections on Israel's War Against the Palestinians*, which found a broad audience and was translated into many languages. After the book, Noam, Ilan, and I continued talking, mostly via emails. One day, during a meeting with Ilan in Brussels, we both came to the conclusion that a follow-up to that book was necessary. One thing that had indeed left me frustrated working on *Gaza in Crisis* was how the email exchanges between Noam and Ilan were not interactive. Noam answered a set of questions, and Ilan did the same. The two authors had no way to respond to or argue with each other.

Ilan and I therefore decided that if another book were produced, it would have to consist of face-to-face conversations. Truly excited by the prospect, I emailed Noam, pretty sure that he was not going to be available due to his extremely busy schedule. To my surprise, Noam responded positively and, a few months after I sent the email, Ilan and I boarded a plane for Boston to meet Noam in his office at MIT.

In preparing the questions and the topics we were going to address, I thought that it was important to start with the past. Some commentators argue that you should always look forward, think about the future, that thinking about the past tends to be a stumbling block that impedes on the negotiations, the peace process. They are, often on purpose, missing the point. The past, as far as Palestine and Palestinians are concerned, is 1948, the *Nakba*, and the ethnic cleansing of two-thirds of the population (yes, two-thirds; try to put this in perspective and do the math with the country you are living in right now) that was expelled from historical Palestine to make space for a new state, Israel. It is a not-so-distant past; we are not talking about centuries ago. It is a very present past, for all Palestinians. Talking about it, analyzing it, is therefore crucial to understanding the current situation. Understanding Zionism is also key and the two professors have slightly different perspectives about the matter.

In discussing the present, we focused on the role of civil society and the impact it can have on radically changing the narrative and actual policies on the ground. The huge growth and the impact of the boycott, divestment, and sanction (BDS) movement cannot be underestimated in putting Palestine back on the map. The BDS movement helped rejuvenate and rebuild the solidarity movement worldwide. It offered a step-by-step guide (with flexibility depending on the different national interests) on how to turn from a defensive stance to an offensive one. The BDS movement asserted: Let's stop trying to justify our actions, let's act. This made for very engaging discussions. The BDS movement is a subject of debate between Professor Pappé and Professor Chomsky and both this book and *Gaza in Crisis* allow room for differences between the two. I do think there is something to gain by enabling this conversation—that it can be constructive and reinforce the struggle for Palestinian rights.

Finally and obviously, we talked about the future—the day-after question. What is actually meant, practically, by a "free Palestine"? What kind of state is possible? Is a state the solution? How will Palestinians and Israelis share the country? What constitution will be drafted?

While it is important to focus on the present, as things on the ground are getting worse every day, having a clear strategy and political vision is crucial if we want people around the globe to see what is possible.

With that, the conversation part was concluded, and, as far as I was concerned, this was good enough. Ilan, however, thought we needed something more. He offered to write what I think is an amazing and incredibly timely and challenging original piece called "The Old and New Conversations." It is a rallying call to move forward, change gears, and totally rethink the vocabulary we use when it comes to the Palestine question—to use semantics as an educating tool for change.

This piece makes, in my opinion, the book a much better and solid one. It fills in the blanks and opens up the debate to the world.

But something brought us back to the present in a most forceful way: another Israeli aggression in Gaza. Shortly after we submitted this book to the publisher, Israel was at it again. "Mowing the lawn" as they horrifyingly call it. The carpet bombing of an imprisoned population by its occupier, with the support of most Western states, spurred Ilan and Noam to write additional contributions. Working on the book again while Israel was indiscriminately carpet bombing a population of 1.8 million Palestinians was often very difficult. When things are radically wrong, writing does not feel like the most obvious response for an activist. Writing while feeling extremely angry and useless often does not produce the best results. I was glad to see some of my close friends involved in civil disobedience actions all over the world. It gave me strength and faith. With good people like that around, the struggle, after all, might not be endless. But the writing was essential and I hope that this book will help challenge the narrative of the powerful, the PR of governments, repeated in loop by the corporate media that helps justify the crimes, that allows them to be committed, that paralyzes people.

The Palestine question is emblematic of what is wrong with the world. The role played by Western states, the complicity of corporations and of various institutions make this case a very special one. The fact that Israel actually benefits from violating international law and receives "red carpet" treatment from the West means that we all have a role to play in ending the injustice that the Palestinians are facing. The injustice in Palestine has ramifications throughout the world. From Ferguson to Athens, via Mexico, it is clear that many governments are reproducing the tools that Israel uses to repress and oppress the Palestinians. The replication of those same tactics, methods, and often weapons serves as proof that the Palestinians are now used as guinea pigs for experimentation. And Palestine is a great laboratory. Exploring the Palestine case is therefore crucial for understanding where we stand as human beings and what we stand for. Finding a solution to this question could then open the door to a new vision, to a new world, to new possibilities for all of us.

Palestine is slowly becoming global—a social issue that all movements fighting for social justice need to embrace. The next step is connecting the dots between various struggles around the world and creating a truly united front.

We are many. We will prevail.

Frank Barat
Brussels
September 2014

CHAPTER ONE

The Old and New Conversations

Ilan Pappé

When Frank Barat and I sat with Noam Chomsky for a long discussion about Palestine we divided our conversation into three parts: a discussion on the past, focusing on understanding Zionism as a historical phenomenon; a conversation about the present, with a particular focus on the validity and desirability of applying the apartheid model to Israel and on the efficacy of the BDS movement as a major strategy of solidarity with the Palestinian people; and finally, in talking about the future, we discussed the choice between a two-state and a one-state solution.

The principal purpose of these meetings was to help us all clarify our views in light of the dramatic changes not only in Israel and Palestine in recent years but in the region as a whole. We assumed that many readers would agree with us that Chomsky's take on Palestine, at the present historical juncture, is a crucial contribution for any relevant discussion on the issue. We hope that this conversation helps to clarify the Palestine issue, specifically highlighting

9

the possible transition that is taking place in the solidarity movement with the Palestinians, with wide implications for the struggle from within Israel/Palestine. We do not cover all the issues; we selected those that seemed controversial, and strove for the exchange to be a civilized one (apart from one or two less-tame outbursts) for a movement that needs to be united. The fragmentation of the liberation movement itself, its apparent lack of clear leadership, and the ambiguity that characterizes the Israeli peace camp all contribute to this dissension. Nonetheless, a dialogue among those who believe in peace must be possible!

We seem to be in the midst of a transition from an old conversation about Palestine to a new one. I myself feel very comfortable in the new conversation but would not like to lose the comrades who are still happier in the older one. So here, in the first part of this book, I aim to delineate the two conversations before engaging in a conversation with Noam on the issues that are at the heart of the matter.

The Old Peace Orthodoxy and Its Challengers

The need to look for a new conversation about Palestine stems first and foremost from the dramatic changes on the ground in recent years. These developments are likely familiar to most of our readers, and I will summarize them in the most updated form possible toward the end of this essay and assess their impact on the future conversation.

But I think the search for new ideas, and maybe even for a new language, about Palestine emerged out of a longer-term crisis. The crisis was characterized by the inability to translate impressive gains outside of Palestine, especially in transforming world public opinion about it, into tangible changes on the ground. The new search is an attempt to deal with several gaps and paradoxes that haunt the solidarity movement with Palestine as a result of this obstacle.

These days the ever-growing camp of activists for peace and justice in Palestine is facing several paradoxes that are hard to reconcile. Let me first consider these paradoxes and then suggest a way forward both through my own analysis, the analyses of others, and finally through a conversation with Chomsky.

The first paradox is the gap between the dramatic change in world public opinion on the issue of Palestine on the one hand, and the continued support from the political and economic elites in the West for the Jewish state on the other (and hence the lack of any impact of that change on the reality on the ground).

Activists for the cause of Palestine sense rightly that their message of justice and their basic understanding of the grave situation in Israel and Palestine are now widely accepted in the world, but yet this has not alleviated the Palestinians' sufferings wherever they are.

While in the past, the activists could have attributed this gap to a measure of sophistication behind the Israeli actions that hid well the uncanny, and quite often criminal, Israeli policies, this could not have been the case in our century. The successive Israeli governments since the beginning of this century rendered any sophisticated analysis of Israel quite redundant. These days, it is very easy to expose not only the Israeli policy but also the racist ideology behind it. The activists' efforts and this deplorable policy produced a dramatic shift in Western, including American, public opinion; but so far this shift has failed to reach the upper echelons of society and therefore on the ground Israel continues—unabated and uninterrupted—its policies of dispossession and does not seem to be paying a price for its policies.

The second gap, indeed paradox, is the one between this widely held negative image of Israel on the one hand, and the very positive image its own Jewish society has of the state. Israel's relative economic prosperity still promises that the most isolated state in the Organisation for Economic Co-operation and Development is regarded by its own Jewish citizens as a thriving state that has ended the Arab-Israeli conflict and has only to struggle with residues of the Western "war against terrorism" in the form of Hamas and Hezbollah (but even that is not deemed a crucial issue in the wake of the "Arab Spring"). Israel does suffer from social and cultural rifts and cracks, but they have been muted for the time being by the invention of a phony threat of an Iranian nuclear war and other such scenarios that also ensure the uninhibited flow of money to the army and security services.

This sense of success of course is not shared by the Palestinian citizens of Israel in the Galilee and the al-Naqab (the Negev) who continue to suffer from expropriation of their land and demolition of their houses and are exposed to a new set of racist laws that undermine their most essential and elementary rights. The Palestinians in the West Bank are still humiliated on a daily basis at checkpoints; arrested without trial, losing their lands to settlers and the Israeli Land Authority; and barred from traveling to nearby villages and towns due to the systems of apartheid walls and barriers that encircle their homes. Those who try pay with their lives or are arrested. And the people of Gaza are still subjected to the barbaric combination of siege and bombardment and shooting in the biggest open human jail upon earth. And of course one should not forget that millions of Palestinian refugees still languish in camps while their right of return seems to be totally ignored by the global powers that be.

The third paradox is that while specific Israeli policies are severely criticized and condemned, the very nature of the Israeli regime and the ideology that produces these policies are not targeted by the solidarity movement. Activists and supporters demonstrated against the massacre in Gaza in 2009 and the assault on the flotilla in 2010, yet in this arena of open and public protest nobody, it seems, dares to attack the ideology that is behind these aggressions. There is no demonstration against Zionism, because even the European Parliament regards such a demonstration as anti-Semitic. Imagine, in the days of supremacist South Africa, if you were not allowed to demonstrate against the apartheid regime itself, but only against the Soweto massacre or any other particular atrocity committed by the South African government.

The last paradox is that the tale of Palestine from the beginning until today is a simple story of colonialism and dispossession, yet the world treats it as a multifaceted and complex story—hard to understand and even harder to solve. Indeed, the story of Palestine has been told before: European settlers coming to a foreign land, settling there, and either committing genocide against or expelling the indigenous people. The Zionists have not invented anything new in this respect. But Israel succeeded nonetheless, with the help of its allies everywhere, in building a multilayered explanation that is so complex that only Israel can understand it. Any interference from the outside world is immediately castigated as naïve at best or anti-Semitic at worst.

These paradoxes at times have frustrated, understandably, the solidarity movement with Palestine. It is indeed difficult to challenge established powers and interests when they refuse to yield to the moral voice of civil societies and their agendas. But there is always a need to think hard about whether more can be done in those spaces and areas in which non-elite groups have the power to impact and change the conversation in effective ways.

In 1982, in the wake of Israel's first invasion of Lebanon, Edward Said wrote an article titled "Permission to Narrate" in which he called upon the Palestinians to extend their struggle into the realm of representation and historical versions or narratives. The actual balance of political, economic, and military powers did not mean, he asserted, that the disempowered did not possess the ability to struggle over the production of knowledge. Whether such producers in, or in the name of, Palestine have heeded Said directly, or were thinking along these lines anyway, this project has indeed begun in earnest. Academic Palestinian historiography and the "new history" in Israel has succeeded in debunking some of Israel's more absurd claims about what happened in 1948 and to a lesser extent had been able to refute the depiction of the Palestine Liberation Organization (PLO) as a purely terrorist organization.

But it seems that the historiographical revision and setting the record right has not had an impact on a peace process that ignored 1948 altogether. The absence of the narrative and the historical conversation about what passes nowadays as a peace process seems to serve the political elites of the day well—on either side of the divide and in the world at large. There is no incentive whatsoever, it seems, to transform the hegemonic discourse that seems to be acceptable exactly because it does not ask for a dramatic change on the ground.

As Said proposed, such hegemony can be challenged by language and narration. We need a more guarded approach when offering this new perspective, as we are not only challenging the hegemonic powers but also the convictions of many Palestinians and genuine friends of the Palestine cause. Hence framing this challenge as a conversation may be more helpful.

I suggest enhancing this conversation by producing a theoretical dictionary, specific to the Palestine issue, that gradually replaces the old one. The new dictionary contains *decolonization*, *regime change*, *one-state solution*, and other terms discussed in the following pages and later with Noam Chomsky and others who try to find a way forward and out of an ongoing catastrophe. With the help of these entries, I hope to reexamine the hegemonic discourse employed by both the powers that be and the solidarity movement with Palestine.

However, before presenting the entries in the new dictionary, I would like to look more closely at the waning of the old one still dominating the conversation about Palestine among diplomats, academics, politicians, and activists in the West. I call this discourse "The Dictionary of the Peace Orthodoxy" (in fact, not my term; but alas I cannot recall where I first heard it and I apologize for justifiable claims of unoriginality).

The Challenge to Peace Orthodoxy

The Dictionary of the Peace Orthodoxy sprang from an almost religious belief in the two-state solution. The partition of the land of Palestine (by allocating 80 percent of the land to Israel and 20 percent to the Palestinians) was thought to be a feasible target that could be achieved with the help of international diplomacy and a change within the Israeli society. Two fully sovereign states would live next to each other and agree on how to solve the Palestine refugee problem and would decide jointly what kind of a Jerusalem there would be. There was also a wish to see Israel more of a state of all its citizens and less as a Jewish state that retains its Jewish character.

This vision was clearly based on the desire to help the Palestinians on the one hand and on realpolitik considerations on the other. It was, and is, driven by oversensitivity to the wishes and ambitions of the powerful Israeli side and by exaggerated consideration for the international balance of power. It is a language born of American political science research and is meant to cater to basic American positions and stances on the issue. Most users of the language that surrounds the two-state solution as the ideal settlement are probably sincere when employing it. This language has helped Western diplomats and politicians remain ineffective—either out of will or necessity—in the face of continuing Israeli oppression. Expressions and phrases like "a land for two people," "the peace process," "the Israel-Palestine conflict," "the need to stop the violence on both sides," "negotiations," or "the two-state solution" come straight out of a contemporary version of Orwell's *1984*. Yet this language is advanced even by people who would find this kind of a settlement morally repugnant (as Noam Chomsky has succinctly put it in the conversation in this book) and unsatisfactory, but who see no other realistic way to bring an end to the oppressive Israeli occupation in the West Bank and the siege on the Gaza Strip. The hegemonic language in the corridors of power in the West and among the Israeli and Palestinian politicians on the ground in Palestine is still that discourse based on the old dictionary.

But this orthodox view is slowly losing ground in the activist world. Granted, the official peace camp in Israel and the liberal Zionist organizations worldwide still subscribe to the view—as do leftist politicians in Europe. In some ways, known and famous friends of the cause still endorse it—some, it seems, even religiously—in the name of realpolitik and efficiency. But the vast majority of activists are looking for a new way out. The emergence of the BDS movement, through the call for such action by Palestinian civil society inside and outside of Palestine, the growing interests and support for the one-state solution, and the emergence of a clearer, albeit small, anti-Zionist peace camp in Israel, has provided an alternative thinking.

The new movement, which is supported by activists all around the world and inside Israel and Palestine, is modeled on the anti-apartheid solidarity movement. This has become clear by the prominence of BDS as the main tactic on campuses during Israel Apartheid Week—*apartheid* now an acceptable and common term used by student activists on behalf of the Palestine cause. This has been followed recently by a scholarly attempt to widen the comparative research on the two case studies, apartheid South Africa and Israel/Palestine, within the paradigm of settler colonialism.

Settler colonialism is a conceptual fine-tuning on the theories and histories of colonialism. Settler movements that sought a new life and identity in already inhabited countries were not unique to Palestine. In the Americas, in the southern tip of Africa, and in Australia and New Zealand white settlers destroyed the local population by various means, foremost among them genocide, to re-create themselves as the owners of the country and reinvent themselves as its native population. The application of this definition—settler colonialism—to the case of Zionism is now quite common in the academic world and has politically enabled activists to see more clearly the resemblance of the case of Israel and Palestine to South Africa and to equate the fate of the Palestinians with that of the Native Americans.

This new model highlights the significant points of difference between the peace orthodoxy and the new movement. The new movement relates to the whole of historical Palestine as the land that needs support and change. In this view, the whole of Palestine is an area that was and is colonized and occupied in one way or another by Israel, and in that area Palestinians are subject to various legal and oppressive regimes emanating from the same ideological source: Zionism. It stresses particularly the link between the ideology and Israel's current positions on demography and race as the major obstacle for peace and reconciliation in Israel and Palestine.

Today it is an easier task to illustrate this fresh point of view. Since 2010, the Israeli legislation in the Knesset—demanding loyalty to a Jewish state from the Palestinian citizens, codifying (thus-far) informal discrimination in welfare benefits, land rights, and job hiring policies against the Palestinian minority—clearly has exposed Israel as an overtly racist and apartheid state. The Green Line that created different classes of Palestinians (those inside Israel and those in the occupied territories) is slowly disappearing because the same policies of ethnic cleansing are enacted on both sides of the line. In fact, the more sophisticated oppression of the Palestinian citizens inside Israel looks at times worse than the oppression of residents living under direct or indirect military rule in the West Bank.

Finally, the new movement does not shy away from pushing forward a solution that is not the preferred one in the eyes of either the Israelis, the Palestinian Authority (PA), or the political elites of the West: the one-state solution. The activist and the scholarly depiction of Zionism as a settler-colonialist movement and the state of Israel as an apartheid state also determine the mechanism of change. For the orthodoxy that mechanism is the peace process, as if Israel and Palestine were once two independent states and Israel invaded part of Palestine, from which it has to withdraw for the sake of peace.

The new approach proposes the decolonization of Israel/Palestine and the substitution of the present Israeli regime with democracy for all. It thus targets not only the policies of the state but also its ideology. From this perspective the Israeli refusal to allow the 1948 refugees to return home is seen as a racist rather than pragmatic position. The new activists voice their unconditional support for the Palestinian refugees' right of return, and they voice it more clearly it seems than some Palestinian leaders.

In other words, the new approach proposes a paradigm shift for the solidarity movement, which hopefully will gain credence among those in power and in particular those who are engaged with the question of Palestine and peace. This new paradigm offers a new analysis for the present situation and proposes a different vision for the future. Many elements in this new paradigm are old ideas that can be found in the PLO 1968 charter and in the platforms of activist groups such as Abna al-Balad, Matzpen, the Popular Front for the Liberation of Palestine, and the Popular

Democratic Front for the Liberation of Palestine. These positions have been updated and adapted to the current reality. The issues brought up in the past by these groups were totally ignored by the orthodox peace movement when it supported at least initially the Oslo Accords in the name of realpolitik. Even at the time that the Oslo process seemed to produce some sort of change on the ground, it was in essence a settlement that ignored the fate of the Palestinian refugees and the Palestinian minority in Israel and did not relate to either the racist nature of the Jewish state or its role in the 1948 ethnic cleansing of Palestine.

The new movement has created a new dictionary that if used extensively can help shift public opinion on the subject. Below are some of the most illustrative and significant entries in this new language used to analyze the situation today in Israel and Palestine and describe a vision for the future. By adopting a new discourse, the activists can strengthen their commitment toward struggling against the ideology behind the current Israeli abuses and violations of human and civil rights, whether they take place inside Israel or in the Occupied Territories.

I have divided the entries into three different temporal zones. One zone relates to the way the alternative activist perspective views the past in general with its particular focus on how to define Zionism and Israel's actions in the past. The second zone relates to the new definition of Israel today, mainly as an apartheid state, and the implications for activism, in particular outside of Israel and Palestine, of such a definition. This sparks a very relevant conversation about the importance and role of the BDS movement and the various Israel Apartheid Weeks held on campuses around the world. The third zone relates to the future—what are the al-

ternatives to the dismal and ineffective attempts to move the peace
process forward on the basis of a two-state solution. This alternative view toward the future substitutes terms such as the *peace
process* with *decolonization* and *regime change* and envisages some
sort of a one-state solution instead of the two-state solution.

These three different perspectives on the past, the present, and
the future were each the focus of the conversations Frank Barat
and I had with Noam Chomsky. We did not choose him as our in-
terlocutor because we think he necessarily represents the "peace
orthodoxy" (although he still subscribes to some of its basic assumptions) but because we feel that his views on these issues are
crucial for pushing forward the discussion on Palestine.

The New Dictionary: The Past

The reassertion of the "Zionism as colonialism" equation is critical not only because it best explains the Israeli policies of Judaization inside Israel and settlement in the West Bank, but also
because it is consistent with the way the early Zionists perceived
their project and talked about it.

The Hebrew verb *le-hitnahel* or *le-hityashev* and the Hebrew
nouns *hitanchalut* and *hitayasvut* were used ever since 1882 by the
Zionist movement and later the state of Israel to describe the
takeover of land in Palestine. Their accurate translation into English
is "to settle," "to colonize," "settlement," and "colonization," respectively. Early Zionists used the terms proudly since colonialism was
very positively received by the public at the time (and continued to
until the end of the First World War). When colonialism's fortunes

changed in the aftermath of the Second World War and *colonialism* connoted negative European policies and practices, the Zionist movement and later the state of Israel looked for ways of dissociating the Hebrew terminology from the colonialist one and started to use more universal and positive language to describe their policies. Despite this energetic attempt to claim that Zionism was not part and parcel of the universal colonialist movement, there was no escape from understanding these Hebrew terms linked to the act of colonization. "To settle" is deemed as an act of colonization in the scholarly and political dictionary of the twentieth and twenty-first centuries. So there is no way out of it: even if the Zionist movement and later the state of Israel did not regard the expropriation of Palestine's land, quite often accompanied by dispossession of the natives, as an act of colonizing, everyone else did.

The analysis through the colonialist perspective also challenges the Israeli claim of "complexity" now desperately used by Israeli scholars to fend off the inevitable comparison between the situations in Palestine and in South Africa. The historical timeline is indeed unusual: it involves a nineteenth-century colonialist project extended into the twenty-first century. But the features and solutions for this project are not unique—it is a simple rather than complex narrative. Although its unique timing would undoubtedly require a complex settlement, the analysis is clear even if the prognosis will demand some ingenuity, since decolonization in the twenty-first century is indeed a complex project.

An important task in this respect is introducing to Western schools' curricula and textbooks this understanding of colonialism and strengthening the research on it in universities. If this were to succeed, the media would follow suit. The task is not easy, but if this message were conveyed effectively, we could then hope that every decent person in the West, as in the time of colonialism, would not stand on the side of the oppressive ideology and instead would identify with its victims and deem their struggle as anticolonialist.

This particular new discourse is likely to be branded by the Israelis as anti-Semitic. But nowadays any criticism, even a soft one, of Israel is regarded by the state as akin to anti-Semitism, so it seems this potential accusation should not dissuade us from using the terminology of colonization. Anyone who does not subscribe to the Israeli version of a two-state solution is suspected of being an anti-Semite. Official Israel demands an absolute support of its version so when powerful secretaries of state do not reflect this version exactly they are condemned as anti-Semites. The Israeli version is a Jewish state next to two bantustans, divided into twelve enclaves in the West Bank, and contained in a huge ghetto in the Gaza Strip, with no connection between the West Bank and the Gaza Strip, and run by a small municipality in Ramallah operating as the seat of government. Official Israel insists that in the interest of national security a Palestinian state, if at all allowed, would be modeled along these lines.

The Present: The Apartheid State of Israel

The scholarly literature comparing the apartheid in South Africa to that of Israel is only now beginning to emerge. Brave scholars such as Uri Davis used the term quite early on. His analysis in the 1980s was the first to expose Israel's land regime and legal practices within the Green Line as another form of apartheid.

Further research has highlighted both the similarities and dissimilarities. It was the first visitors from post-apartheid South Africa, who together with former US president Jimmy Carter, frequently used the term. Although it seems from very early on that they realized the regime imposed on the Palestinians in the West Bank and the Gaza Strip was in many respects far worse than that of the apartheid in South Africa.

The most recent research has noted how uniform Israeli legal, economic, and cultural policies have become on both sides of the Green Line. The de facto and more invisible apartheid has been replaced by racist legislation in the Knesset and open policies of discrimination. It may be a different version of apartheid, but the Israel of 2014 is a state that segregates, separates, and discriminates openly on the basis of ethnicity (which in American parlance would be race), religion, and nationality.

Since the reference to apartheid has become common in the corridors of power as well as among activists, one can see why the inventive group of activists in Canada who initiated Israel Apartheid Week on their own university campus inspired so many others in the world to follow suit. The phenomenon has become so widespread (now also in Israel and Palestine) because it resonates with what people knew is happening on the ground due to the growth of the ISM (the international solidarity movement). It has provided an alternative source of information to the distorted reports of the mainstream media in the West, in particular grabbing public attention in the United States when Rachel Corrie, a young activist in the ISM, was brutally killed by the Israeli army.

The Apartheid Weeks are the main focal point of annual activity for the cause in Palestine and they have won over the campuses that were previously dominated by Zionist lobbying and academia. Because of the kind of harassment Steven Salaita, Norman Finkelstein, and others endured as university appointees suspected of harboring pro-Palestinian views, college professors and staff are still concerned in the United States that they too may be subjected either to a prolonged process of promotion or be disqualified and refused tenure. But the trend in the other direction is growing and campus communities as a space of debate have become more hostile toward those who support Zionism and more friendly to those who wish to show solidarity with the Palestinian cause. This has not transformed yet into support from university administrations, but the tide is definitely moving in the right direction.

The analysis of Israel as an apartheid state that resembles South Africa during its worst moment has produced another prognosis that is diametrically opposed to the raison d'être of the "peace process." Most of the whites in South Africa were still quite racist when their regime of oppression collapsed, which means that change did not come because they were transformed from within the country. They were forced to change by the African National Congress (ANC) struggle and international pressure. While activists still struggle in and outside of Palestine to emulate the unity and power of representation the ANC enjoyed, they can more easily see how to manage a campaign of pressure from the outside inspired by the anti-apartheid movement with South Africa. The new basis for such activity is a realization that the change will not come from within Israel.

This is how the BDS campaign was born—out of a call from Palestinian civil society to pressure Israel through these means until it respects the human and civil rights of Palestinians wherever they are. The campaign, which in many ways became a movement, has its problems. The absence of clear representative and effective Palestinian institutions has forced the activists to act within a leadership vacuum. Hence at times strategic decisions have seemed to overstep the boundaries of what is tactical. The campaign's relationship with boycott initiatives on the ground (such as the boycott of settlement goods in the West Bank or the rejection of any normalization with Israelis) is not always clear. But these flaws pale in comparison to the campaign's success in bringing to the world's attention a crisis that is at times overshadowed by the dramas that have engulfed the region since 2011. Major companies have rethought their investments in Israel, trade unions have ceded their connections with Israeli counterparts as have various academic associations, including leading ones in the United States, and an impressive number of artists, authors, and world-renowned figures, including Stephen Hawking, have cancelled their trips to Israel.

One component of the campaign—the academic boycott—is still contentious as is clearly evident in the conversation Frank and I had with Chomsky (Norman Finkelstein also publicly condemns this tactic). But it seems that it is accepted by many others as part of the new dictionary of activism and recently led to the creation in Israel of a "committee of boycott from within," made up of Israeli Jewish academics with impressive membership numbers.

The Present: Ethnic Cleansing and Reparations

Insisting on describing what happened to the Palestinians in 1948 and ever since as a crime and not just as a tragedy or even a catastrophe is essential if past evils are to be rectified. The ethnic cleansing paradigm points clearly to a victim and offender and more importantly to a mechanism of reconciliation.

It clarifies the connection between Zionist ideology and the movement's polices in the past and Israeli policies in the present: both aim to establish a Jewish state by taking over as much of historical Palestine as possible and leaving in it as few Palestinians as possible. The desire to turn the mixed ethnic Palestine into a pure ethnic space was and is at the heart of the conflict that has raged since 1882. This impulse, never condemned or rebuked by a world that watched by and did nothing, led to the massive expulsion of 750,000 people (half of the region's population), the destruction of more than five hundred villages, and the demolition of a dozen towns in 1948.

The international silence in the face of this crime against humanity (which is how ethnic cleansing is defined in the dictionary of international law) transformed the ethnic cleansing into the ideological infrastructure on which the Jewish state was built. Ethnic cleansing became the DNA of Israeli Jewish society—and remains a daily preoccupation for those in power and those who were engaged in one way or another with the various Palestinian communities controlled by Israel. It became the means for implementing a not yet fulfilled dream—if Israel wanted not only to survive but also to thrive, whatever the shape of the state, the fewer Arabs in it, the better.

Ethnic cleansing motivated not only the Israeli policy throughout the years against the Palestinians but also toward the millions of Jews who were brought from Islamic and Arab counties. If they were to partake in the Zionist dream, they had to be de-Arabized (losing any connection to their mother tongue and proactively showing how un-Arab they were by daily expressing their self-hate, as Ella Habib Shohat has put it, for everything that is Arab). The Arab Jews who could have been the bridge to reconciliation turned out to be one of the highest obstacles to it.

Ethnic cleansing's most preferred method is expulsion and dislocation, but in the case of Israel this was not always possible. This limitation forced the Israelis to be quite inventive in finding other means to continue with the vision of an Israel that has an absolute Jewish majority in it. They found that if you cannot expel someone, the second-best option is not to allow him or her to move. Enclaving people in villages and towns and disallowing any spatial expansion of human habitats became the hallmark of Israel's ethnic cleansing after 1948, and it is still used today very effectively. When asked to explain why one new Palestinian village or town was not allowed to be built between the River Jordan and the Mediterranean (a prohibition benefiting the other ethnic group that today constitutes half of Palestine's population), the official Israeli line is that Palestinians do not need the same space as Jews do and are quite happy to be stuck in their homes without free access to green spaces around them. In the past, any short aerial tour over the West Bank would have shown you how Palestinian villages used to look—comfortably spread over the hills of eastern Palestine, beautifully mingling with the natural landscape. But they have been gradually strangulated, especially if they lie in the vicinity of Jewish settlements or are locked between them, as is the case in the Galilee. At the same time the Jewish settlements, on both sides of the Green Line, form a very spacious suburbia.

So the refusal to allow the repatriation of refugees, the military rule on the Palestinians who were left inside Israel (1948–1966), the occupation and treatment of the Palestinians in the West Bank, the erection of the apartheid wall, the silent transfer of Palestinians from Jerusalem, the siege on Gaza, and the oppression of the Bedouins in the al-Naqab are all either stages or components in an ongoing ethnic cleansing operation.

Using the term *ethnic cleansing* is also about justice. At every given moment in the history of the conflict, justice was ridiculed when it was even suggested as a principle in the attempts to solve the conflict. *Ethnic cleansing* however ensures that the basic right of return for those who were expelled is not forgotten, even if it is constantly violated by Israel. It seems that no real reconciliation will be possible without at least recognizing this right.

A new dictionary of activism is based on applying the universal concepts advanced by reparations to the case of the Palestinian refugees. The international community has long ago established the mechanism for treating the victims of ethnic cleansing, and reparations is often used as the remedy and solution. Reparations here exist in a spectrum of possibilities to allow the victims and the victimizers to build a new life. These possibilities include the physical return of those who survived ethnic cleansing or financial compensation to those survivors who wish to build a new life elsewhere. It also includes mechanisms for reintroducing the victims in the country's historical accounts and retrieving their cultural assets. The major point of all these mechanisms is that it is up to the victims of the ethnic cleansing to decide individually which reparation they would prefer.

But there is more at stake here than just defining and properly conceptualizing the reparation paradigm as part of the new rec-

ommended dictionary. The idea of reparations, and in particular
the right of the refugees to return, is rarely questioned in any other
conflict in the world, apart from Palestine. The European Union
and the US State Department have a principled position on
refugees that accepts without any hesitations or qualifications the
right of people to return to their homes after fighting has subsided. The United Nations has a similar universal position and
made a concrete decision on the right of the Palestinian refugees
to return unconditionally to their homes when it adopted Resolution 194 in December 1948 (it was adopted by the same UN General Assembly that decided on the partition plan and the creation
of the Jewish state).

So putting the right of return at the very heart of any future solution is not a revolutionary idea that asks the Western world to
betray its principles or adopt a unique exceptional attitude. On
the contrary, it requires the Western world to be loyal to its principles and not exclude the Palestinians from the application of
those principles. Yet the old peace orthodoxy abandoned these
basic human principles and did not even think of fighting for
them. Well, the new movement does and will put them at the
center of its struggle as long as the last refugee wishes to return.
The Al Jazeera "Palestine Papers" leak exposed how far the Palestine Authority was willing to go in order to appease the Israelis. It
showed the PA's readiness to give up this right of return. The new
realities described at the end of this section reveal the emergence
of a new political elite in Palestine that may have a different view
on the issue.

Finally, this ideology of ethnic cleansing also explains the dehumanization of the Palestinians—a dehumanization that can

bring about the kind of atrocities we witnessed in Gaza in January 2009. This dehumanization is the bitter fruit of the moral corruption that the militarization of the Jewish society bore in Israel. The Palestinians are a military target, a security risk, and a demographic bomb. This is one of the main reasons why ethnic cleansing is an ideology that is regarded by the international community, in the aftermath of the Second World War, as a hideous crime and moreover one that can lead to genocide—since with both crimes you have to dehumanize your victim in order to implement your vision of ethnic purity. Whether you expel or massacre people, including children, they have to be objectified as military targets, not as human beings.

Anyone who has been in Israel long enough, as I have, knows that the worst corruption of young Israelis is the indoctrination they receive that totally dehumanizes the Palestinians. When an Israeli soldier sees a Palestinian baby he does not see an infant—he sees the enemy. This is why all the military documents, whether those ordering the occupation of villages in 1948, those instructing the air force in 2009 to resort to the Dahiyah Doctrine (the strategy that was meant to defeat Hezbollah in the 2006 assault on Lebanon with the carpet bombing of the eponymous southern suburb of Beirut, which is the Shiites' stronghold), or when bombarding Gaza, depict the civilian areas as military bases. In Israel, since 1948, ethnic cleansing is not just a policy—it is a way of life, and its constant practice criminalizes the state, not just its policies.

More important, when one has such a term in the activist's dictionary, he or she realizes that ethnic cleansing does not end because it peters out. It ends either when the job is completed or is stopped by a more powerful force.

This realization turns on its head the logic of the peace process that has been attempted so far. The process was meant to limit the implementation of Israel's policies onto the pre-1967 borders. It has not of course succeed in doing that, as the basic Zionist quest is for control, direct or indirect, over the whole of Palestine. Any tactical concessions on this space have been only due to demographic considerations, not a desire for peace and reconciliation. For this reason, the direct control over the Gaza Strip has been abandoned and the Zionist Left supports the two-state solution. But this course of action is not working and as the recent, more direct ethnic cleansing operations of Israel in the Negev, the Jordan Valley, and the Greater Jerusalem area have shown, the old plan A—of direct expulsion—is still used in order to complete the work that was begun in 1948.

Thus, the peace process forces Israel to be more inventive in its ethnic cleansing strategy but does not require it to stop that strategy. The new dictionary regards the end of the ethnic cleansing as a precondition for peace.

The depiction of Zionism as colonialism, the analysis of Israel as an apartheid state, and the recognition of how deeply imbedded the notion of ethnic cleansing is in Jewish society in Israel is the source of thee key entries in our new dictionary shaping our view of the future: *decolonization*, *regime change*, and a *one-state solution*.

The Future: Decolonization and Regime Change

The invalidity of the term *peace process* in regards to the Israel/Palestine conflict became clear when people started to have access to what was really happening on the ground. Through the work of the ISM, as well as communication via the Internet, satellite TV, and other means, people in the West could see the discrepancy between the various attempts to solve the conflict (such as Geneva 1977, Madrid 1991, Oslo 1993, and Camp David 2000) and what was really taking place on the ground. In this respect Chomsky was the first to observe that the process was never meant to reach a destination but only to perpetuate a situation of no solution. Israel used it as a means to grab more land, build more colonies, and annex more space. The status quo was the solution.

The entry of *decolonization* in the dictionary would hopefully put an end to the "coexistence" industry, which fueled a false dialogue financed mainly by the Americans and the leaders of the European Union. Most Palestinians have pulled out of this post–Oslo Accords project and wasted millions of dollars.

What was particularly annoying and unhelpful was the paradigm of parity on which the peace process was based: it divided the blame between the two parties and treated them as equally responsible for the conflict while offering, allegedly, an equitable solution. The blatant misbalance of power should have discredited this solution a long time ago as a realistic approach to peace. It was based on the wish to appease Israel without irritating it too much. The end result was that the Palestinians were to receive whatever Israel was willing to give them. This had nothing to do with peace; it was a search after a comfortable capitulation by the native people of Palestine who lost it to the Zionists who invaded the region in the nineteenth century.

But the new dictionary is not made of entries based on romantic or utopian notions. Past injustices cannot all be undone; this is very clear to the people who have been branded as "unrealistic" even by their friends. Not all past evils can be rectified, but ongoing evils surely should stop. And this is where the entry *regime change* becomes so appropriate.

According to the new movement it is not unthinkable to aspire to a regime change in Israel, nor is it naïve to envision a state where everyone is equal. And it is not unrealistic to work for the unconditional return of the Palestinian refugees to their homes. The principle of regime change was abused by the United States and Britain in their attacks on Iraq and Afghanistan but won a new international legitimacy in the popular revolutions in Tunis and Egypt.

Regimes can change dramatically and drastically, but they can also change gradually and in a bloodless manner. Although the upheavals in ex-Yugoslavia and Syria serve as warnings of how badly regime change can go, most of the historical examples in recent times are of nonviolent, or nearly nonviolent, regime changes. Therefore, the last entry in the new dictionary, a *one-state solution*, is based on the hope that a clear vision of how the future relationship between victims and victimizers is framed will indicate also the nature of the change needed and the way to achieve it.

For many activists the two-state solution was dead long before the desperate admission of that fact by US secretary of state John Kerry in April 2014. The strengthening of voices about the demise of the settlement does not mean that a clear alternative immediately has emerged. A long process in search of the alternatives has just begun. Some people, activists, and new political organizations have already articulated a clearer program and idea of what such a state would be. Their views are based both on old ideas that were developed in the past and their own new inputs. Others are still groping in the dark. But the journey has commenced.

Preliminary milestones of this journey have been achieved. The first milestone was the reconceptualization of Israel and Palestine as one country—not two present or future states. Palestine became once more a country called Palestine and not just a geopolitical reality called Israel and the Occupied Territories. And it is in this space that the new dictionary needs additional entries to clarify how people who live in Palestine, and those who were expelled from it, could live as equals and even live in ways better than in other parts of the Middle East, maybe even better than in some parts of Europe.

A second milestone, which was particularly crucial (as again can be gleaned from the conversation with Chomsky in the second part of this book), was the refutation of the allegation that the one-state vision denies Israel's right to exist. The new movement of activists does not possess the power to eliminate states nor are they interested in doing so. Israel has the power to eliminate states; the peace movement does not. But it does have the moral power to question the ideology and ethical validity of the state and the destructive impact it had through the expulsion of half the country's population.

The third milestone was the head-on challenge of one of the most basic assumptions of the peace orthodoxy: that partition of a country is an act of peace and reconciliation. Partition in the history of Palestine is an act of destruction committed within a framework of a UN "peace plan" that drew no international reaction or condemnation whatsoever. Thus the terms in the international dictionary from that formative period that signify positive peaceful values such as partition are a newspeak, to borrow George Orwell's famous term for such deceptive realities. Partition signifies international complicity in the crime of destruction, not a peace offer.

Consequently, anyone opposing partition became the enemy of peace. The more sinister and pro-Israeli elements of the peace orthodoxy used to blame the Palestinians for being irresponsible, warmongering, and intransigent—beginning with the Palestinian rejection of the partition plan in 1947. In hindsight, we know partition was also an ill-conceived idea from a realpolitik point of view. This may not have been known at the time. But to offer partition now as a solution on the same premise that informed the 1947 resolution—which was that Zionism was a benevolent movement wishing Israelis to coexist as equals with the Palestinian native majority—is an absurdity and a travesty.

The continued adherence to the interpretation Zionism gave to partition, and liberal Zionism very recently gave to the Oslo process, corrupts every human and humane value cherished in the West. Partition, in both 1947 and 1993, means a license to have a racist Jewish state in more than 56 percent of Palestine in 1947 and more than 80 percent, if not more, in 1993.

This is where the senior Israeli and pro-Israel Western political and social scientists are exposed in their utter immorality and indecency. They claim, and teach, that a Jewish state reigning over much of Palestine, provided there is a Palestinian entity next to it, is a democratic reality. It is a democracy that is maintained by all means possible to ensure an everlasting Jewish majority in the land. These means could and have included genocidal policies and other brutal strategies to safeguard that the state embodies the ethnic identity of one group alone.

Israelis do not find it therefore at all bizarre or unacceptable that determining the results of a democratic process by first determining by force who makes up the electorate gets the desired result: a purely Jewish state in a binational country. This charade is still marketed successfully in the West: Israel is a democracy because the majority decides what it wants, even if the majority is determined by means of colonization, ethnic cleansing, and, recently, by ghettoizing the Palestinians in the Gaza Strip, enclaving them in Areas A and B in the West Bank and in isolated villages in the Greater Jerusalem area, the Jordan Valley, and the Bedouin reservations in the Naqab.

Israeli Jews need to safeguard the existence of the Palestinians, threatened daily by their government and army, before nourishing the project of coexistence. If they want to help, they can join the international solidarity movement and those within the land who wish to transform Israel and Palestine into a geopolitical entity in which everyone can live as equal persons and citizens.

Conclusions: Palestine and Israel, 2014–2020

In order to move out of the paradoxes mentioned above, the ideas of the old peace camp have to be abandoned. The international community interested in helping Palestine needs to stand behind the attempt to turn Israel into a pariah state as long as Israel continues to pursue its policies of apartheid, dispossession, and occupation.

The peace process between Israel and the Palestinians is a medical miracle: it died several times, was resuscitated for a while, then collapsed again. It holds on not because there is the slight chance it will succeed but because of the dividends its very existence brings to many involved. The Israeli government understands that without this "peace process" Israel would become a pariah state and would be exposed to international boycott and even sanctions. As long as the process is alive, Israel can continue to expand its settlement project in the West Bank and the dispossession of the Palestinians there (including in the Greater Jerusalem area) and establish facts on the ground that would render any future settlement unfeasible and impossible. Because of the dishonest brokering of the United States and Europe's impotence in international affairs, Israel continues to enjoy immunity in this process.

The Palestinian leadership is divided on the question of how desirable the continuation of the process is. Senior members in the Palestinian Authority assert that the establishment of the PA was a very important national achievement and therefore should be maintained. Others, and it seems this includes President Mahmoud Abbas himself, have begun to doubt the validity of the PA and the chances of reaching peace. It is true that hollow threats to "hand over the keys to the Israelis" were voiced in the past by Abu Mazen, in order to exert pressure on Israel; but it seems that the threat from Israel in spring 2014 was more genuine and the sense of despair more real. And therefore the attempts to establish a unity government with Hamas, which were resumed in earnest that April, may have a better chance of succeeding.

The new efforts at unity were just one indication that quite a few of those who supported the process in the past, and those who have been observers, have prepared themselves for the eventuality that the medical miracle would not repeat itself and the dead would not be resurrected. Most of those who try and understand as well as predict what will take place, if indeed the process cannot be revived, see any other alternative as disastrous. The Zionist Left as well as liberal pro-Zionist bodies in the West talk about the "nightmarish" scenario of a binational state, not only because it would mean the end of Zionism but also would produce a far worse reality for both peoples (as if things can get worse for the Palestinians).

The Israeli Zionist Left has a bizarre explanation for its fear of a binational state, or for that matter of a single democratic state. The Palestinians will become "tree hewers and drawers of water," as the biblical phrase has it, proponents warn us (a warning made several times by Uri Avnery). Others describe scenes of a never-ending civil war. Among the Palestinians the support for the two-state solution comes from a different angle. It is perceived as the only settlement that has global support, even inside Israel, and therefore should still be maintained. Quite a few of Palestine's genuine friends continue to subscribe to this point of view for similar reasons.

Although the way the center and right wings in Israel imagine a two-state solution differs from that imagined among members of the Zionist Left, or within parties such as Hadash and Tajamu' in Israel, and differs again among PA members and supporters of Palestinians in the enlightened world, there is generally a consensual depiction of it that dominates the political conversation on Palestine in the world.

But will the consensus be there in 2015? More and more voices among various Palestinian communities and among non-Zionist Jewish activists are replacing their unwavering support for the two-state solution with a search for new alternatives.

It is on the ground that one can see clearly how irrelevant this hegemonic and orthodox discourse of peace is and how futile any future attempts to revive it will be. The Zionist Left has disappeared from the political scene in Israel for all intents and purposes, and thus the only viable political alternatives are either a coalition between the Right and a secular Center or a coalition between the Right and ultra-orthodox Jews. The emergence of a new and left-leaning political force in Israel does not seem likely at this time. Anyone who is still hopeful of such an eventuality underrates the mental process Jewish society in Israel underwent following the creation of the state in 1948. It was put under an indoctrinating steamroller that pressed together old Jewish phobias about hostile Gentiles in Europe with typical colonialist anxieties about the natives into a frightening local version of racism. Deep racist layers like this are not removed easily and definitely do not disappear by themselves as the case of post-apartheid South Africa has so clearly shown us.

Counter-educational projects in the long run, active resistance, and huge pressure from the outside can transform a society like that in Israel. However, counter-education is a very long process, and the immediate dangers emanating from the collapse of the diplomatic effort have such destructive potential that they would render these educational efforts useless. As for the resistance movement, it is still fragmented (it has produced five different Palestinian groups that developed discretely since 1948, each with its own national agenda) and has to navigate in an almost impossible historical reality. Forging unity is another long-term process, probably taking as long as it would take to immunize Jewish society against the racist virus that affects it. The BDS movement with all its incredible achievements—and there are many—has still not affected the political elites in the West who are still providing Israel with immunity for its actions and policies.

In spite of positive developments—a few brave Israelis seek to confront their society's racism in all its political manifestations (a systematic policy of ethnic cleansing in the Negev, Jaffa, Acre, Nazareth, East Jerusalem, the Jordan Valley, and south of the Hebron mountains) and its constitutional manifestations (a racist wave of legislation in the Knesset); the BDS movement becomes stronger by the day; and we may be witnessing genuine efforts at Palestinian unification—on the ground a new state, the Greater Israeli state, has been born. This state has nearly completed the annexation of Area C in the West Bank and offers the Palestinians in Areas A and B incarceration in cages if they do not resist the new state or the threat that they will be treated like the population in Gaza if they do resist. This model is offered to the Palestinian people throughout the new state. In cages there is no room for spatial expansion, no resources for development and progress, and an absolute prohibition on resisting this new vision of a greater Israeli state.

Whoever follows the index of racism and democracy in Israel recognizes this is a creeping reality—a slide toward an age of more racist legislation, expanded projects of Judaization, and an alarming increase in attacks on Palestinians under the slogan *Tag Mehir* (Price Tag) that consists of the daily destruction of Palestinian property and holy places. In the new Greater Israel, impotent local Palestinian councils and uninterested police forces watch helplessly as organized crime takes over the more deprived Palestinian neighborhoods and villages between the River Jordan and the

Mediterranean, fed by the poverty and unemployment that has reached unprecedented levels.

This is a tough reality that could be and should be challenged, but it is left intact partly because of the energy wasted in the futile peace process, as well as in power struggles among its victims over insignificant fiefdoms.

Today, in three areas a new conversation has to commence that addresses, rather than ignores, the reality. The first area is the overall Israeli policy that has obscured the Green Line, already in existence for many years, and which basically treats all the Palestinians in the same way. There are still advantages for Palestinians who are citizens of the state of Israel, but these seem to disappear as the years go by. As mentioned before, this is happening not only because Israel is less interested in providing these advantages but also due to the growing recognition that a hidden apartheid system, such as the one in Israel itself, is no less oppressive than a direct occupation (in the West Bank) or prolonged siege (in the Gaza Strip).

When different forms of oppression emanate from the same source, the struggle against it has to be focused. I have no illusions that in the near future we will all be guided by a clear and unified Palestinian strategy, but whoever subscribes to the importance of the Jewish-Palestinian joint struggle has to recognize a worldview that confronts the ethnic cleansing throughout all of Palestine and not just in part of it. A genuine and clear conversation about the new options instead of a dead formula is imperative at this moment in history. The reframing of the Arab-Jewish relationship over the whole land of historical Palestine is a crucial project that has to commence. Whatever one proposes in terms of the future political entity, it has to be based on full equality for whoever lives in or was expelled from the country. Each such entity or ideal future model hopefully could be developed through the existing representative bodies and new ones that might emerge. But for the sake of some sort of progress beyond the conceptual paralysis imposed on us in the name of the two-state solution, anyone who can and wants to—on every possible stage—should offer a political, ideological, constitutional, and socio-economic structure for whoever lives in the country of Palestine—and not just in the state of Israel.

The second area is the future of the Palestinian refugees. As long as this question is discussed within the framework of the old peace orthodoxy and the two-state solution discourse, it remains marginal and its solution deemed possible only as a return of refugees to the future Palestinian state. A totally different conversation about the refugee issue focuses on two subjects: the first, an analysis of the Israeli refusal to allow the return of refugees as yet another manifestation of how racist this state has become; the second, the need to consider the fate of the refugees in the light of the new refugee problem in Syria (which includes large numbers of Palestinian refugees).

Within the framework of the diplomatic effort that was based on the two-state solution, Israel's determined rejection of any return was legitimized, as was the Israeli argument that return would not allow Israel to maintain a Jewish majority in the state. This international legitimacy indirectly licenses Israel to employ any means it deems necessary to maintain a significant Jewish majority in the state. In this respect there is no difference between an Israeli position that rejects the refugees' right of return and the other Israeli projects of ethnic cleansing, be it proposing to annex

Wadi Ara to the West Bank, uprooting the Bedouins in the Naqab, or depopulating East Jerusalem and the Jordan Valley. Peace cannot be on the agenda of a state that exercises such policies against its own citizens. A subject associated with the refugee question is the immediate fate of the Palestinian refugees in Syria, Lebanon, Iraq, Turkey, and Jordan who fled the civil war in Syria. Israel boasts of its humanitarianism by telling the world that it admitted dozens of wounded Syrian fighters to its hospitals. But Syria's four neighbors, who have no less complicated relationships with Syria, absorbed *hundreds of thousands* of refugees. Even if Israel does not show any humanitarian interest in these refugees, many of whom are Palestinians, anyone who is part of the peace camp inside and outside Palestine has to highlight the linkage between the Syrian tragedy and the Palestine issue: the need to offer the old-new Palestinian refugees a return to their original homeland has to be endorsed as both a humanitarian gesture and as a political act that can contribute to the end of the conflict in Israel and Palestine.

The right of return in general should be placed at the heart of much of the activity inside Israel (and there are early encouraging signs that the local agenda of activists there is moving in this direction). The Nakba took place where Israel is today, not in the West Bank or the Gaza Strip. Any conversation about reconciliation with both communities should take this fact as a starting point. A preliminary step is probably recognizing at least the right of internal Palestinian refugees (about 250,000 today by conservative estimates) to return to their homes or nearby. The right of internally displaced persons to return is the issue on which the widest consensus can build inside Israel in the struggle against the ongoing ethnic cleansing. The internal refugeehood presents a testimony from the past for what, and against what, the struggle is all about. The refugees are already part of the demographic balance. How these people will return and how other refugees will return is a question that has to be at the center and not on the margins of the public debate about Palestine in this century.

The third and last area is the absence of any socialist discourse from the conversation about Palestine. This absence is one of the main reasons the so-called peace camp in Israel (and the same is true regarding the lobbyists on J Street in the United States) has no issue with neo-liberalism. This worldview is not opposed to Israeli withdrawal from the Occupied Territories but has no position on the harsh economic and social oppression that does not distinguish between a West Bank inhabitant and an Israeli citizen. It is true that, unfortunately, some of the Jewish oppressed classes in Israel, in particular the Arab Jews, who see themselves as Jews first, subscribe to extreme racist views, but their plight is another good reason not to give up on a worldview that challenges the present economic, not just political, regime between the River Jordan and the sea.

The absence of this angle also weakens our ability to understand the Oslo Accords, the creation of the PA, projects such as People to People, and the maintenance of the occupation by EU and USAID money as neoliberal projects. Economic elites supported the "peace process" because it was perceived to lead to an economic bonanza.

The importance of insisting on a socialist worldview can be gleaned from the example of post-apartheid South Africa, which has proven so disappointing as it maintains an economic structure that still discriminates against the African community there. Those who represent institutionally, collectively, or individually this worldview have a responsibility to make sure the conversation about it will not stop at the Green Line but will relate to Palestine as a whole; and who knows, it may kick off a serious conversation about the future of the Middle East in its entirety.

Heading toward 2020, we will all most probably face a racist, ultra-capitalist, and more expanded Israel still busy ethnically cleansing Palestine. There is however a good chance that such a state will become a global pariah and the people around the world will ask their "leaders" to act and end any relations they have with it. What they should not hear are the past slogans, which are no longer relevant in the struggle for a more just and democratic Palestine.

PART ONE

Dialogues

CHAPTER TWO

The Past

Frank Barat: How important is the role of the past in understanding the present? More and more, people are asking the Palestinians to move on—to forget about the past, the Nakba of 1948, the refugees. How would you respond to that?

Noam Chomsky: Well, it's not just on this issue. It's quite standard for those who hold the clubs to say: "Forget about everything that happened and let's just go on from here." In other words, "I've got what I want, and you forget what your concerns are. I'll just take what I want." That's what it translates as—in this case too. To forget about the past means forgetting about the future because the past involves aspirations, hopes, many of them entirely justified, that will be dealt with in the future if you pay attention to them. It's essentially saying, "Let's dismiss just hopes and aspirations because we've got what we want."

Ilan Pappé: I definitely agree with this. I would say that in the case of Palestine, and why we continue to receive requests to speak and

This conversation between Noam Chomsky, Ilan Pappé, and Frank Barat was recorded on January 14, 2014, and has been condensed and edited.

give our views, the clock of destruction continues at every historical juncture at a much faster pace than our clock of ideas on how to get out of this. This stalemate continues however because the perception of those who manage the so-called peace process—those who interpret the reality in Palestine and Israel and claim that they know what is the right solution—is rigid and has not changed for years.

At its base is a formula for peace that insists on taking the past out of the equation of peace. These peace brokers claim that the relevant past for any peace process is the moment the process begins. Anything that happened before is irrelevant for that process. So if you already have huge Jewish settlement blocks all over the West Bank, you cannot think about dismantling them. You may think about the exchange of territories but not about dismantling these settlements. So the past becomes an obstacle in the eyes of the so-called mediators, but the past is everything in the eyes of the occupied and the oppressed people.

NC: I might add to that it's universal. President Obama says: "Well let's forget about the crimes that were committed, the invasion of Iraq, let's just go on." In others words, let's continue the same way we've been proceeding. That's the weapon of the powerful.

IP: Absolutely.

FB: Zionism has become a word that has many definitions and interpretations. Some people don't know what it means anymore. Could you give us an overview of what this word has meant historically?

IP: As you're saying, Zionism has many interpretations. Its more neutral definition would be ideology I suppose. Zionism is a set of ideas that inspires people to do certain things and act in accordance to them. What is important in my mind is how people in power interpret this ideology. I'm less interested in how it is interpreted by neutral scholars. I'm interested in Zionism as an ideology that has an impact on people's lives on the ground. As such, it is an ideology, and has been, since almost the beginning of the Zionist project in Palestine, that meant, in very simple terms, that Judaism as a national movement has the right and the aspirations to have as much of Palestine as possible with as few Palestinians in it as possible. Such a reality was determined as a precondition for creating new Jewish life. I think that throughout the years, when you have an institution like a state, which accepts this ideology as its ethical infrastructure, that ideology becomes even more powerful in the life of people.

As such it is not that different from other national or cultural ideologies. Its uniqueness lies elsewhere. Zionism today is an ideology of power that is quite peculiar in history as it is directed against one particular group of people. Usually ideologies have wider implications for people. Zionism is very focused.

[Whether it can] be substituted by a more progressive ideology is a very good question. The best way forward seems is for its victims and opponents to see how far they can progress, motivated by a set of universal values of human rights and civil rights. Because most of what is interpreted today as Zionism violates, and contradicts, basic human rights and civil rights for anyone who is not a Jew in Israel. Rather than finding the alternative ideology as such, the goal is to create positions that claim the right of people to elementary human and civil rights.

FB: Is there a clear definition of Zionism today? What is a Zionist today?

NC: First of all I think that here again the past is relevant. Zionism meant something different in the pre-state and post-state period. From 1948 on, Zionism meant the ideology of the state. A state religion. Like Americanism, or the magnificence of France. In fact even in this period the notion has changed. I remember for example in 1964, I happened to spend some time in Israel, and among leftish intellectuals, Zionism was regarded as a joke. A thing that was used for propaganda for children. Three years later, most of these people were raving nationalists. That changed in 1967, which was a sea change in the way many Israelis saw themselves and what the state was like. Fundamentally in the pre-state period it was not a state religion. For example, in the mid-1940s, I was a Zionist youth leader, but strongly opposed to a Jewish state. I was in favor of Jewish-Arab working-class cooperation to build a socialist Palestine, but the idea of a Jewish state was anathema. I was a Zionist youth leader, because it was not a state religion.

You go back a bit further, my father, his generation, they were Zionists, but they were Ahad Ha'Amists. They wanted a cultural center as a place where the diaspora could find a way to live together with the Palestinians. That ended in 1948. From then on, it essentially became a state religion. One that shifted, in terms of policies. It's interesting to remember this. In the mid-1970s, it was clear that the Arabs were perfectly willing to make a political settlement. Syria, Egypt, and Jordan proposed a two-state settlement at the Security Council; the USA had to veto it. Egypt had already offered a full peace treaty with Israel. It was necessary to raise barriers to block negotiations. So the concept of Zionism changed. Everyone had to accept the "right to exist" of Israel. States do not have a right to exist. Mexico does not accept the right of the USA to exist sitting on half of Mexico. States recognize each other but not their right to exist. There is no such thing.

But Israel raised that barrier to require that Palestinians accept that their oppression and expulsion is justified. Not just that it happened, but that it is justified. Of course they are not going to accept that. So it was a nice barrier to stop negotiations. Now it's harder. The support for a settlement is now so overwhelming that Israel has been forced to raise the barrier still higher. The Palestinians now have to recognize Israel as a Jewish state. That's the core element of most of the speeches that Netanyahu gives. Why that? Because that's understood to be impossible. Nobody should recognize Israel as a Jewish state. Just as we do not recognize the USA as a Christian state. Say Pakistan calls itself an Islamic state, but the USA does not recognize it as one. Zionism in the policy of the state of Israel has had to shift to impose still higher barriers to any kind of political settlement. If something more is needed in the future, they will invent something new. Zionism as state policy is a shifting concept depending on what the state needs.

IP: For me there is one constant dimension of Zionism that does not easily shift with time, one can call it mainstream Zionism, sometimes referred to as Labor Zionism. It's the colonialist, or settler-colonialist, dimension of Zionism. From the moment the more vague ideas of Zionism as the revival of Judaism as nationalism became the concrete project of settling in Palestine, Zionism became a settler-colonialist project and still is one today. Maybe the means of colonizing Palestine are changing according to circumstances and the balance of power, but not the vision itself. Within that act of colonizing also come perceptions of the native, or the indigenous, population as being an obstacle for the success of the project. I think that this part of Zionism stays at the heart of the ideology even before the state was founded. The state just enhances the ability to colonize but does not change the vision of colonizing Palestine.

Palestinian perspectives on it, however, did change with time. Noteworthy is the position of Palestinian intellectuals and leaders such as Azmi Bishara, who argues that the settlers today have a certain right and presence in Palestine. When the first wave of settlers came as Zionists, it happened at a historical moment when quite often in the history of nineteenth-century colonialism, the local population could opt for resistance and successfully, usually in an armed struggle, push the colonizers back to their home countries. When the colonizers are already a third generation and even succeeded in founding their own state, the native population has to strategize differently and find ways of coexisting with this generation of colonizers.

The reason the colonialist impulse of the Zionist movement did not end at a certain historical moment lies in the territorial appetite and greediness of these settlers. When they were offered part of Palestine in 1937 they regarded it as insufficient space for implementing their aspirations. But they had a wise leader, David Ben-Gurion, who understood that it was tactfully beneficial not to spell out clearly these annexationist dreams. So he told the Royal Peel Commission the Zionist movement was content with a small part of the country.

He continued this tactical and successful policy in 1947 and led his community to accept a larger part of Palestine than that offered in 1937, but one that he still deemed as insufficient. He told his colleagues he was very unhappy with the map offered by the UN Partition Plan in November 1947 and promised them, as indeed happened, that they would have the means, the opportunity, and the plan to change these borders later on. His successors still hope to re-create his winning formulae today after Israel completed the takeover of the whole of Palestine in 1967. But unlike Ben-Gurion in 1937 and 1947, they so far failed in obtaining the international legitimacy for the last territorial expansion (and unlike him at least some of them were even seeking, again unsuccessfully, Palestinian legitimacy for this act).

NC: I think that's a correct characterization of what you'd call hard-core Zionism or more generally political Zionism, which of course Ben-Gurion was a leading figure of. But Zionism generally was broader. Like Ahad Ha'Am was a Zionist, but not a political Zionist. The groups that I was involved in admittedly were marginal. Like Kalvarisky's League for Arab-Jewish Rapprochement. They were Zionists, but anti-state. They were class based and in favor of Jewish-Arab working-class cooperation. It might sound strange today, but it did not in the context of the thirties and the forties.

IP: The Jews were a minority then. Is it possible when the Jews are a majority and in power to develop such ideas?

NC: Well this is later. A majority and a state. In fact they were strongly opposed to it at the time. So the concept changed. What you are describing is a correct characterization of the mainstream of political Zionism. Technically the Zionist movement did not formally accept the notion of a state until 1942, but it was always in the background of political Zionism. You just could not say it. I think it's worth thinking through what the options were because that may be some kind of a guide to what the future could be.

FB: Nowadays a lot of people describe Zionism as a settler-colonial movement. Do you both agree with this definition?

NC: The Jewish settlement in Israel was certainly a settler-colonial movement. When you talk about what Zionism was, it depends on how wide you want to spread it. The movement that developed, yes, is a settler-colonial society. Like the USA, Australia, the Anglosphere. Israel is one of them. It's not a small point. If you take a look at the international support for Israeli policies, it's of course primarily the USA, but secondarily it's the Anglosphere. Australia, Canada. . . . I suspect that there is a kind of intuitive feeling on the part of the population. Look, we did it, it must be right. So they are doing it, so it must be right. The settler-colonial societies have a different kind of mentality. We did exterminate or expel the indigenous population so there has to be something justified about it—superior civilization or other ideas.

IP: Our chance to change international perspective and perceptions even in settler-colonialist societies has to do with the past. Even if you go to the USA and Australia nowadays, maybe because the policies were genocidal and happened many years ago, I do not think these societies will resort easily today to settler-colonialist practices. They may deal well, or not so well, from our perspective, with crimes of the past. They may find different ways of engaging with them. As the Australians did when they initiated the Sorry Day. Or even a more progressive act of reconciliation in the permit given by the government of New Zealand to the Maoris to return to their lands that were stolen from them. All these acts are taken from what one can call the comfort zone of those settlers' societies that have diminished the native population to such an extent, at the early stage of colonization, that they have no fear the symbolic acts will change the socio-economic or even political realities of today. For the Israelis, of course the task is far more formidable. They are still dispossessing because they failed in the early stage of the 1948 ethnic cleansing to eliminate the Palestinians as a people. And thus every symbolic act of reconciliation would have a profound and tangible impact on the socio-economic and political realities on the ground. Most Israeli Jews do all they can to prevent this from happening. Where they are not sure about their success is in winning international and regional legitimacy for their acts.

NC: It's true. Israel has had the problem that it's a twentieth-century version of a seventeenth- through nineteenth-century colonialism. That's a problem. But my point was a little bit different. There is a kind of an underlying mentality in the Anglosphere, in settler-colonial societies, which is simply some kind of deep-seated part of the way in which people look at the world and that slips through. However, speaking about the future, this is changing in the Anglosphere. Since the 1960s, mainly the effect of sixties-era activism, there has been a considerable revival, a significant one, of concern for what actually happened in the past. A lot of it was suppressed until then, literally. You go back to the 1960s when leading anthropologists were claiming that there were maybe only a million Indians [Native Americans] around the country. That's collapsed. Now attitudes are very different. I think this is part of the background for the increasing criticism of the settler-colonial character of Israel. These things are connected in sort of subtle ways.

IP: I agree and I think that this shift in perceptions in the settler-colonial societies is something we are still struggling with as activists. I remember how I struggled to explain to my students in England that what they see in Israel and Palestine today is a daily implementation of nineteenth-century colonialist ideology and discourse.

NC: Yes.

IP: Where the Israelis find it difficult is actually in escaping the description of the reality as colonialist when trying to do this in Hebrew. Any translation into another language of the Israeli terminology of settlement is bound to expose the colonialist nature of the project. Even those progressive Jews who support Israel feel uncomfortable when this act of translation is taking place.

This Israeli predicament is also our predicament as activists. We are dealing with a nineteenth-century fossil that is very alive and kicking in the twenty-first century. That's why I think the power of connecting the past to the future comes through the paradigm of settler colonialism. Because settler colonialism is not only about the act of settling and colonizing but what happens afterwards.

NC: Driving out the indigenous population.

IP: Exactly.

FB: I want to go back to the question of a Jewish state. If the Jews are a people, what is the problem of them having a state? And why shouldn't we recognize Israel as a Jewish state?

IP: I think that no one I know has ever objected or questioned the right of people to redefine themselves on a national, ethnic, or cultural ground. There is no ground for objecting from the perspective of international law or international morality. Neither is the historical moment in which they decide to do it questionable, however this particular group had defined itself in the past (in our case, as a religious group).

The problem lies elsewhere. What is the price paid by this transformation and who pays the price? If this new definition comes at the expense of another people, this becomes a problem. If a group is a victim of a crime and is looking for a safe haven, it cannot obtain this by expelling someone else, another group, from this space that you want as your safe haven. This is the difference between what you want as a group and what means you use to achieve it. The problem is not the right of the Jews to have a state of their own or not. That's an internal Jewish problem. Orthodox Jews might have a problem with this. Palestinians have no qualms about the Jews forming a state in Uganda, as some people proposed in 1902 to 1903. Not one Palestinian in the world would be interested in this scenario. That's the main issue. How do you implement your right to self-determination?

NC: The idea of a Jewish state is an anomaly. It's not something that's happened somewhere in the world. The question is based on the wrong presupposition. Take France: It took a long time for France to become a state. A lot of violence and repression took place. In fact all state formation is a process of extreme violence. That's why Europe was the most violent place in the world for centuries. Once a state is established, any citizen is a citizen of the state. No matter who you are, if you are a French citizen, you're French. If you live in Israel, and you are an Israeli citizen, you are not a Jew. So the Jewish state concept is a complete anomaly. It has no analogs in the modern world. Therefore it's obvious why we should not accept it. Why should we accept this unique anomaly?

Every state, if you look at its history, is created by extreme violence. There is no other way to impose a uniform structure on people of varying interests, backgrounds, languages, and so on. So it's done by violence. But once it's there, at least in the modern state system, anybody who is part of a state is theoretically an equal member of the state. Of course it might not work in practice, but that's the concept. In Israel it is totally different. There is a distinction between citizenship and nationality. There is no Israeli nationality. You cannot be an Israeli national. This came up in the courts back in the sixties and came back up again recently. A group of Israelis wanted to have their papers identify them as Israelis, not as Jews. It went all the way to the high court, which rejected it. It reflects this anomalous concept of a Jewish state, which has no counterpart in the contemporary international political system.

IP: Paradoxically it is used by Israel in an attempt to stifle any criticism of the state and its ideology. If you chastise Israel, you assault the Jewish state and by association you attack Judaism. That's a very interesting line of argumentation and defense.

This prohibition would not work in any case. If you look at the struggle against apartheid in South Africa, it is as if in the heyday of the struggle against apartheid, you were only allowed to criticize certain policies of South African society but not the very nature of the regime. That's a great success for Israel that it obtained immunity from such a protest movement so far. They defined the parameters of the game: you are allowed to demonstrate against Israeli policies, but if you demonstrate against Israel, you demonstrate against the Jewish state and therefore you demonstrate against Judaism. That is why it is very important to bring this to the fore of the discussion.

NC: It's interesting that it is now the Israeli leadership itself that is bringing it to the fore.

IP: Exactly.

NC: When Netanyahu says, "You have to recognize us as a Jewish state," he is saying: "You have to recognize us as something that does not exist in the modern world." There is no such thing. Again, if you are French, a citizen of France, you are French. If you are a citizen of Israel, you are not Jewish. It's crucial.

FB: Could Israel have formed without the Holocaust?

NC: It's hard to debate such a question, but I think it would have. What Ilan was describing before, the national institutions that had been created—they were strong, there was a military force, an ideology, support for it in the powerful countries, for all kind of reasons. Like in Britain and in the US, a lot of the support for it was religious. Christian Zionism is a very significant force. It goes back way before Jewish Zionism. It was an elite phenomenon. Lord Balfour, Lloyd George, Woodrow Wilson, Harry Truman read the Bible every morning. It says there, "God promised the land to the Jews." That's in the powerful states. There was already plenty of support. In fact, Britain as the mandatory authority facilitated the development of the Jewish national institutions. So my guess is that it would have happened without the Holocaust.

Also it's worth remembering that the Holocaust was not a big issue in the 1940s. On the contrary; it became a big issue after 1967. If you take a look at the Holocaust museums, the Holocaust studies programs, it's post-'67. It's very striking in the USA. So ask yourself a very simple question. After the war, there were many survivors of the Holocaust, many of them living in concentration camps. They were in camps that were essentially no different from

the Nazi extermination camps except that there were no cremato-
ria. There were US government presidential studies that investi-
gated and said that the people were living under the conditions of
Nazi occupation. Simple question. How many of them came to
the United States? Virtually none. If you had asked them where
they wanted to go, I think you can make a sane guess that they
would have wanted to come to the United States. Half of Europe
wanted to come, especially Holocaust survivors. They did not.
The American government did not want them, the American
Jewish community did not want them. Zionist emissaries took
over the camps. They had a principle that able-bodied men and
women between seventeen and thirty-five had to be shipped off to
Palestine. The first book on this, which has been a suppressed
topic, appeared a couple of years ago, a Yosef Grodzinsky book.

IP: Only in Hebrew, right?

NC: It's in English too. But it's been so suppressed that nobody knows about it. It's deeply hidden but it does exist. The
translation of the Hebrew title is "Good Human Material." The
idea was that the good human material was going to be cannon
fodder. Nobody studied it, but you can be pretty sure that coming
to the US was what they would have chosen. That's what the
Holocaust meant. You can see it in propaganda. Truman is very
much honored because he was trying to force the British to send
Jews to Palestine. Nobody asks why Truman did not say, "Okay,
let's take a hundred thousand Jews here." This is the place where
it would have been easiest to absorb them. It can absorb anybody.
It's a country that is not densely settled, the richest country in history. . . . They did not because the Holocaust was considered a
way to damn the enemy, but it was not a meaningful concept.

When the first scholarly study of the Holocaust came out, by Raul Hilberg, it was condemned. "Let's not bring out all that stuff; we do not want that."

IP: I do agree, though I have a slightly different take on this. It has a lot to do with historical timing. It is absolutely true that without the Holocaust there were vested religious and strategic Western interests to have a Jewish presence instead of a Palestinian one, or they would have called it at the time an Islamic one. You particularly see it when you read the correspondence surrounding both the Balfour declaration and its aftermath in Britain in the 1920s and 1930s. A few British public figures were trying to protect the interests of the indigenous Palestinians, but already then they were saying that it was almost impossible to bring the other point of view to the public's attention. You were immediately stifled and rebutted and so on. It was not just Christian Zionism alone that won the day for Zionism long before the Holocaust. The impulse to allow, indeed to push, Jews to settle in Palestine was motivated also by British, and Western, Islamophobia.

NC: True.

IP: It was anti-Arab, anti-Muslim. If you take a place where Christian Zionists or secular British imperialists want to see Jewish presence, serving their empires or theologies, and do not wish to see there an Arab or Muslim presence, it becomes a powerful international coalition that defeats a priori the indigenous people. This was the powerful coalition the Palestinians had to face when they first attempted to create a national movement and struggle for their right of self-determination and independence.

The Holocaust had an effect on the historical timing. But I think that the historical timing is important. After the Holocaust there is the beginning of historical processes by which the power of Islamophobia or Arabophobia, or Christian Zionism, wanes. Call it the Left, call it progressiveness—these forces eventually decolonized the Arab world and even Africa. So Zionism without the Holocaust could have found it a bit more difficult to establish what it did establish in the same place it did.

NC: I totally agree with this.

IP: What Noam said about the DPs (displaced persons) is very interesting because when both the Anglo-American commission in 1946 and we can see it from Richard Crossman's memoirs and both UNSCOPs (United Nations Special Committee on Palestine) afterward in 1947, when they tried to be sort of neutral, and said let's see both sides' points of view on Palestine, many members of both committees claimed that visiting the DPs, of course with good Zionist propaganda, made them associate the fate of the Jews of Europe—demographically, arithmetically—with the fate of the Jews in Palestine. Which put the Palestinian point of view in a very weak position. Who are you to be against our wish to solve the problem of the Jews in Europe as a whole? You could not visit Vienna in 1900 and ask the Jews to come to Palestine. It would not have worked then.

NC: You're right, but I think it tells you something very interesting about Western culture. When they went to the concentration camps and were appalled, they did not say, "Let's save the survivors"; they said, "Let someone else pay for saving the survivors."

IP: Exactly.

NC: This tells you something about the West, the deeply rooted imperial mentality that affects the West like a plague. Yes, there are these people living in misery. We are the ones able to help them, but we are not going to even raise that possibility. Somebody else, who does not have the capacity, they have to suffer for it.

FB: Was it only due to imperialist policies or also due to Western anti-Semitism?

NC: Zionists or not, they would have reacted exactly the same.

IP: I agree.

NC: Take say the USA, which is the clearest case. After the Second World War, they were in an absolutely unique position. There was some Zionist pressure, but it did not mean anything. They just did not want them, and the American Jewish community did not want them either.

FB: Was it anti-Semitic?

NC: Anti-Semitism partly, but mostly, "Why should we take the burden?"

IP: Not them and not anyone else. It did not have to be Jews.

NC: In 1924 there was an immigration law in the USA that was aimed at Jews and Italians. Let's keep them out of the country. They did not say it that way, they said Eastern and Southeastern and Southern Europeans.

IP: The pathology of Zionism is crucial. When you are a historian you always have to remember that people did not know what was going to happen. So when you look at Zionist discussions in the 1930s about Nazism and fascism. You have to realize that these people are talking about Nazism without knowing what will be the "final solution." They are not appalled. They say that they should talk to these people. "We have a uniformity of interest here." They want the Jews out of Germany, we want the Jews out of Germany. On this basis they even go into negotiations. You do not correlate Zionism with Nazism when you say that. You show that you are in the company of people, and they had to understand which interests they were serving apart from theirs. This comes to the fore very strongly.

NC: It's very striking. It's important to stress that in the 1930s you could not see what was going to happen. It was even true of German Jews. There is a book in 1935 (by Joachim Prinz, *Wir Juden*). This is a humanist Zionist who said that Jews should recognize that they should be sympathetic to the Nazis because they have the same kind of ideology we do. Blood and land and so on. We agree with that, if we can only explain to them that we are really on the same side, they will stop persecuting us. This was in 1935. In fact you can go to 1941, the USA had a consul in Berlin, prior to Pearl Harbor, and he was writing fairly sympathetic commentaries on the Nazis. His name was George Kennan. One of the framers of the postwar world.

IP: Yes, Kennan, the strategist who thought that America should control 50 percent of the world's natural resources to have the standard of living they desired.

FB: The refugee question is key for any Palestinian—inside or outside Palestine. Don't you think that the first step the Israeli government should take is to accept its responsibility in creating the problem in the first place, and then, as Kevin Rudd did in Australia, issue a public apology? Also, should we, as activists, clearly state that regardless of the possibility or not of the refugees and their descendants going back to their original homes, they do have this right?

NC: I think that not only they should do it, but it's come close to that. There has been among the various informal negotiations like Geneva, a move to say okay, let's admit that they have the right of return, while recognizing that they will not return. To use an analogy, I gave a talk in Arizona recently and I simply referred to it as occupied Mexico, which it is. It should be referred to that way. It's occupied Mexico. We conquered it in a violent brutal war of aggression. We should do something about it. That's why they have names like San Francisco, San Diego, Los Angeles, and so on. Recognize it, recognize what we did. On the other hand we know we are not going to give it back to Mexico. There are terrible historical injustices, some of them you can try to do something about, but just to unwind history is very difficult. Maybe in the longer term this could happen in Israel. In fact in my view the only way there would be a realistic solution to the return problem is if the whole state system erodes in the region. If you travel in the northern Galilee you can see that there is no basis for a line there.

I'll tell you an anecdote. In 1953, my wife and I were living in a kibbutz in Israel, we were students, hiking around, backpacking in the northern Galilee. On a road behind us a jeep came by, a guy came out and started yelling at us: "You have to go back, you are in the wrong country!" We crossed into Lebanon. These days it's probably bristling with machine guns. There should not be any line there. Over time I think there is a chance that these borders may erode. The whole Sykes-Picot imperial arrangement is beginning to erode. And it could go further, in the longer term. When they talk about a two-state solution, I do not think that this should be regarded as the end. As I've said before, states have no inherent legitimacy. They have all been imposed by violence, they are causing violence all over the world. It's an inhuman social structure. It should erode every time. In that context I think you could imagine an authentic return. Not just recognition of an historical wrong, but in fact interactions among people that are not based on states or religious or ethnic lines. There are other grounds for people to interact with one another.

IP: Well, I do agree with most of it but I think that there are three dimensions to this question. One is tackling it as key issue in the peace negotiations. The right has symbolic and practical aspects. There is a Palestinian demand for an Israeli recognition of the right itself through a combination of acknowledgment and apology. This, maybe in the form of an apology, can open the ground for discussions over practicalities.

The second dimension is the implication of the Israeli position on the very nature of the state and the Zionist project. The Israeli rejection of the right of return stems from a racist ideology; hence for me as an activist, struggle over, or engaging with, the issue of the right of return relates directly to the question of the moral validity of Zionism and the nature of the Jewish state today.

NC: Yes.

IP: The reason they do not accept the return has nothing to do with practicalities. It has to do with Jewish supremacy and Jewish exclusivity.

NC: Yes.

IP: So you struggle against it from an Israeli Jewish perspective not so much on the level of acknowledgment and apology, which I think are important for the peace process to progress, but on this whole other level.

The third dimension concerns the Palestinians alone. It concerns the question of how to live an ordinary life under the shadow of the "right of return" slogan. How does one navigate between perceiving the right as sacred with the knowledge it is not around the corner? This translates into concrete questions: Do you really condemn Palestinians in the refugee camps in Lebanon for improving a little bit their homes, without immediately accusing them of naturalization (*tawtin*)? Or that they have betrayed the right of return because they have slightly improved their standard of living? It's up to the Palestinians to strategize, I am not going to do it for them. But they will have to strategize and differentiate between for instance refugees in the West Bank, the Gaza Strip, the internal refugees inside Israel, and also the refugees in Jordan, Syria, and Lebanon.

These three dimensions are very important for developing a novel approach toward this painful issue. For me, the basic point is: What is a Jewish state? Can it really exist as such? What would be a solution that is not based on a continued violation of basic human and civil rights and one that has to include the right of people to come back to their homeland, their right to visit their homeland? I think that's where we sometimes do not differentiate between what is right, what we believe is justified, and what should be the issues we discuss inside Israel, inside the Palestinian community, and among the community of negotiators and mediators. We should be beyond that argument of supporting or not the right of return. We should talk about what it means. This is what Israeli society has to do. Have a serious internal discussion about its own racist nature.

NC: In support of the observations that it is really a racist issue is the fact that Israel has been trying to block by law or by force commemorating the Nakba or recognizing it.

IP: Exactly.

NC: This has nothing to do with refugees, this is pure racism. Justifying your own repression and violence. I was in refugee camps not that long ago. The people live in horrible conditions. It's very moving. I visited a family who lived in a small room. As usual, Middle Eastern–style, they offered coffee and so on, but when they start showing you the keys of their villages, their houses, pictures of their land, when they start telling you idealized stories about what life was like in the Galilee . . . you're right, Ilan, it has to be dealt with realistically, but it's hard to tell people like that, "You are never going to see your village again."

IP: No, you should not say that. What I meant is that we should tell them that until they see their villages, they should make their lives better. You are not undermining your chance of seeing your village by creating some comfort in your life now.

NC: That's right.

IP: You are not undermining your life as a Palestinian citizen of Israel by pushing aside accusations of practicing normalization because you have a Palestinian theater in Haifa. Such a theater was accused of *tabi'* (normalization) for accepting a budget from the Israeli Ministry of Culture. In Israel you can open a theater in Haifa without taking money from the ministry. These issues, living life under slogans [having moral or political purity], have a lot to do with the fact that if you are struggling for a different moral infrastructure for a future state, it would be far more important to provide a different ethical base for this future state to which the refugees would return. Whether it is one state, a federal state, a binational state, if you fight for a different ethical infrastructure for the state, the whole issue of people wanting to change their lives, either by coming back or by visiting, becomes a different issue.

The conversation here is different and we do not condemn people for persisting in the last sixty-five years to dream about their return home. They have this right. But what do we do until that right is implemented? To my mind this is no less important than protecting the right.

NC: At a human level, some steps should be taken. Like the Israeli women who bring Palestinian women to the beach. It's very important. I mean, imagine those people that can see the sea but cannot touch it—the fact that there are some efforts to overcome that. That's the way things could begin.

FB: I remember, Professor Chomsky, that you told me in a previous interview that Israeli policies will lead Israel to self-destruction. The issue, for example, of bringing as many Jews to Israel as possible, regardless of their "real" Jewishness. Russian Jews, Ethiopian Jews . . . the internal racism it creates, between Haredi Jews, Ashkenazis, Mizrahis . . . is becoming very worrying and problematic. Can you reflect on that?

NC: That's one kind of problem, internal. But what I had in mind was a different one. In 1971 Israel made a decision, which in my view was its most fateful decision in its history. There was an offer from Egypt for a full peace treaty. The Israeli government, led by Golda Meir, considered it and rejected it because they wanted to colonize the Sinai. Basically their choice at the time was between security and expansion. A peace treaty with Egypt, whatever one might think about that outcome, would have meant security, in fact, permanent security as Egypt was the only powerful Arab military force. They understood that, but they preferred to expand into the

Sinai. This was a fateful decision and it's been followed ever since. Ever since then Israel prefers expansion over security. To say they prefer expansion to security means that they are going to follow the path of apartheid South Africa because that follows automatically. Step by step they are going to become isolated, a pariah state, delegitimized, very much like South Africa, they are going to be able to survive only as long as the US supports them. It's very interesting to look at the history of South Africa. You could pretty much replace the word *South Africa* with *Israel* all through the history.

Back in 1960 roughly, the apartheid regime recognized that it was becoming an international pariah. We now know from declassified documents that the foreign minister called the American ambassador and told him that he knew everyone was voting against them, but that as long as the US was backing them, they did not care. That's pretty much what happened. By 1988 and a few years beyond, the US was still supporting South Africa, strongly. Thatcher too, but it was mainly Reagan and the US. South Africa was okay. When US policy shifted, apartheid ended. Israel is moving in exactly the same direction. By now, their sole support, virtually, is the US. They are becoming delegitimized. They are worried about it, but it is going to continue. It's inherent with a policy of expansion, disregard of international opinion, violations of international law, you can get away with it as long as you have the biggest thug on the block protecting you. But that's a weak support because it is going to erode in the US too, just like it did with South Africa. You can already see it happening. The US anti-apartheid movement really started in the eighties, twenty years later than it did in England. But it did develop and it was significant and it changed policy.

IP: I think that what you are saying is correct. To a certain extent there is one big difference between South Africa and Israel. Usually people that do the comparison say that unfortunately it will be much more difficult to dismantle Israeli apartheid than the South African one.

NC: It's not apartheid, I think the state is going to collapse.

IP: It is a demand for a regime change.

NC: It's very different from apartheid. It's really an issue of delegitimization and isolation.

IP: What I am saying is that the white community in South Africa was, from a socio-economic point of view, quite homogenous. Whereas the white supremacist group in Israel is polarized economically and socially. If you add to this what Noam was talking about, the international delegitimization of Israel, you have two powerful processes. One from the inside and one from the outside that really questions the viability of the state. If you belong to the master race, but within the master race you have such a polarization in how the economic cake is being shared, you are in trouble.

The Israelis now have to brand two commodities. They have to market to the world the legitimacy of the state in a world that finds it very difficult to accept it. But then they have also a domestic branding to do. They have to explain to the poor and marginalized Jews why belonging to the master race has not improved their socio-economic standards of living. Why do they still live in impoverished development towns? Why is their culture not represented in the European-dominated and hegemonic culture? Israeli strategists will tell you that they have dealt with this by having a common enemy, a security issue, by having a war on Islam. The explanations and excuses have changed with time, but the polarized socio-economic reality remained the same. That's where the Israelis will find it difficult. There is a limit to how much you can justify a socio-economic marginalization and polarization. This became a more acute problem because since 2008, the middle class in Israel is being pushed down to being the lower middle class, which means that a larger number of people is prevented from getting its share of the national cake despite their belonging to the "right" ethnic group.

In the past and until recently, the ability to keep enough people convinced that their ethnic association also benefits them economically depended largely on the huge amounts of American financial aid to Israel. It is not very clear how much longer such massive aid will be continued. The tendency to review critically how much America is spending abroad does not come only from anti-imperialist critiques in the United States, and the people who would demand a reduction in the aid to Israel are not necessarily pro-Palestinians. The question would be whether the Jewish state is still a strategic asset or financial liability.

These processes will work to weaken the Zionist state in the long run. But my great fear is about the near future. As I heard and learned from veteran ANC leaders and activists, the apartheid regime became particularly fierce and vicious in its last years. It is the prospective fall of Zionism that brings us to a very dangerous period in the history of Palestine. We all have to be very alert and on guard about what is going to happen in the next few years rather than in the long term. You can be a bit more optimistic about the long term in terms of justice and changes in the reality.

NC: I would not push the South African analogy too far because there are striking differences. One difference that cannot be acknowledged in the USA for obvious reasons is that it was the Cubans that destroyed the South African regime. It was they who drove South African aggressors out of Angola, Namibia, broke the mythology of the white superman. It was Black troops that were driving them out. It had an enormous effect. It is going to take a long time before this enters the US consciousness. The other thing is what you talked about. The homogenous white community. Which meant that there was a crucial class issue. It was possible to reach a settlement in South Africa the kind of which is impossible in Israel. The final settlement was, let's keep the socioeconomic system and have some Black faces in the limousines. You cannot do that in Israel.

IP: Making the parallel between South Africa and Palestine has advantages and disadvantages. You already have a Palestinian bourgeoisie inside Israel. You did not have African heads of medical departments in South Africa. Take the Galilee for example. There the intertwined communities are slowly becoming a fact of life. It already has a reality that reflects the future. The nature of the state is still ethnic and segregationist, but the transition to a state that recognizes the reality that already exists on the ground does not have to be as dramatic or drastic as it was in South Africa. In other parts of the country, especially in the West Bank and Greater Jerusalem area, dismantling the present reality and replacing it by a more just one would be very similar to the process occurring in the transition in South Africa from apartheid to a post-apartheid state. So there is no harm is studying closely the South African case so as not to repeat the mistakes made there and also be aware of the differences that would require original thinking for the case of Israel and Palestine.

NC: South Africa was different because the white population needed its Black counterpart. It was its workforce. Israel does not want the Palestinians. South Africa actually supported the bantustans. They wanted them to develop because they had to reproduce the workforce and to be internationally recognized. In details it's not going to be a similar process even though there are some similarities. What I mentioned before—Israel determined that they will be a pariah state, but that it did not matter as long as the US backed them. That's very much the South African position. That is why I have often written, since the 1970s, that the people who call themselves supporters of Israel are in fact supporters of its moral degeneration and probably ultimate destruction.

IP: Absolutely.

CHAPTER THREE

The Present

FB: What is the role of activists standing in solidarity with the Palestinian people? Should they be pragmatic in terms of their advocacy or should they lead the way and adopt more ethical and radical positions? Should we focus on occupation or on the nature of the state of Israel?

NC: If their goals are to help the Palestinians, while they should of course take positions that are ethical, they also must be pragmatic. They have to ask themselves what is going to help and what is going to hurt the Palestinians. Take the antiwar movement about Vietnam for example. There were young people who were properly outraged by the war and thought that the ethical attitude to have was to carry out acts of destruction against US property, corporations, destroy armaments, and so on. That's ethical, but it was harmful. The Vietnamese were strongly opposed to it. They did not care about the fact that people in the US felt good, they cared about what happened to them, on the ground. And the

---

This conversation between Noam Chomsky, Ilan Pappé, and Frank Barat was recorded on January 17, 2014, and has been condensed and edited.

effects on them were harmful since it provoked a huge backlash and strengthened support for the war. Those are the kind of choices that you always have to make when you are considering acting in the interest of someone. You have to ask what is going to help them, not what is going to make me feel good. Call it pragmatic if you like, but I would call it ethical. You are concerned with the effects of your actions on the people you are standing in solidarity with.

Look at the South African solidarity movement. They actually lived up to this condition pretty effectively. By and large, looking at their actions, they selected actions which both harmed South African apartheid and enhanced support for the anti-apartheid struggle in their home countries. That's what we should be doing. And that can be done. Take Israel, a couple of days ago we read a report about settlements in the Jordan Valley, which have had their profits reduced by European boycott movements. That doubly makes sense. It harms the occupation and it is quite intelligible to the audience at home. It's an educational process. You are trying to get people to understand that these are criminal activities and that you are using creative ways to undermine those activities. Those are the kind of actions that make sense. There are other actions that are harmful. First because they have almost no effect on the policies, but they also predictably create a backlash of opposition which simply strengthens the crimes. For example, ten years ago, at the time when Sharon invaded the West Bank and there were these massive atrocities in Jenin, there were protests here. There was a faculty petition condemning it. I signed it mainly out of sympathy for the people who were doing it, but I thought it was badly designed. It had provisions in it which were guaranteed to be unintelligible to the general population and to create a backlash. They insisted on including something about the fact that the university should divest from Israel. No background was laid for that. Nobody understood why. Why not divest from Harvard? The result was exactly as I thought. There was this huge reaction dwarfing the petition. For the next couple of months the issue at Harvard was not Jenin; this was forgotten. The issue became is there anti-Semitism at Harvard. So then you spend a couple of months arguing about that. The net effect for the Palestinians was predictably harmful. These are the type of things you have to think about. You have to ask what the consequences are going to be for the victims. That should be the highest priority all the time. Tactical decisions are important. They are not trivial. Human lives depend on them.

You have to think carefully about what the effects are and the multiple dimensions involved. One, what does it have to do with the policy of the state; how does it affect that? The other is, what about the audience here—at home—that you are trying to mobilize to become more active themselves, through civil disobedience and everything else? There are people who I very much respect, mostly religious Christians, who are very dedicated. They think it's very important to break into military installations and smash all these kind of missiles. I can understand why they are doing it. But the net effect turns out to be predictably harmful. For one thing, the workers in the plants have no idea what the protesters are doing except taking their jobs away. No background has been laid explaining why they are breaking the missiles. There are no educational efforts in the community to make people understand that this is something sensible to do. The net effect is that you spend enormous amounts of time and money wasted in court cases, testifying and so on, and then a couple of people go to jail, and nothing has been achieved. Those are the kinds of questions you have to ask all the time.

IP: I think there are three elements here which are very important to consider: the fragmentation of the Palestinian existence; the accountability of the Zionist ideology for the reality we face today in Israel and Palestine; and finding the right balance between ethical positions and concrete actions.

The first point is to relate to the biggest success of the Zionist project, which was to fragment the Palestinian existence; in this respect they suffered more than the Vietnamese or the South Africans (although not in terms of human cost, at least in the case of the former). The Palestinians have gone through history ever since 1948 as a fragmented group and thus different Palestinian groups are exposed to a ton of different Israeli policies. As an activist, when you have a fragmented group with no clear leadership, no clear address to which you can refer to get clear guidance of what are the national priorities of the people you support—it is not always easy to come with the right or adequate response. In other words, it is very difficult to adopt a clear ethical position that respects the interests of all the Palestinian groups concerned. For instance it is obvious that when you live under occupation in the West Bank or when you are a refugee in Lebanon you may have different priorities as far as the Israeli policies against you are concerned, and therefore you would ask the solidarity movement to do two different, contradictory, things.

The second point is the role and accountability of Zionism. I think what activists were looking for is a kind of framework which tried to contain as many of the Palestinian communities of suffering as they could. Knowing that in some cases, some policies will be less adequate for one group, and more adequate for another. This is where I see activism doing the right thing in the last few years, where it takes Zionism not so much as an ideology or a scholarly riddle that has to be deconstructed, but refers to it mainly as the source of most of the evil that torments Israel and Palestine. The Palestinians are subjected to different sufferings because of Israeli policies, but there is an ideological source behind it.

Sticking to such a framework as activists is highly important to my mind. As I have pointed out earlier there is anomaly in the way Zionism has been until now protected from any serious challenge or rebuke. Activists in the West were allowed to demonstrate against apartheid in South Africa, and did not limit their actions against just one or other policy of the South African government. There is a greater willingness among activists to confront the ideology behind the policies.

Finally there is the need to strike the right balance between the ethical positions and concrete actions. At the end of the day it is the concrete actions of the activists that help the people on the ground. But this is not always easy to do. This is one of the predicaments facing the BDS movement. The campaign can be very helpful when it is focused on the evils perpetrated in the occupied West Bank and the besieged Gaza Strip. But this is also a movement that galvanized thinking people from all walks of life who do not want to support just one particular Palestinian group but would like to face the oppression, and violation of human and civil rights, wherever it occurs and point to its source.

It is of course important to maintain the general discussion the BDS campaign has generated about Israel's nature and policies and to use it when it can be helpful. I can give two different recent examples to show the different roles BDS can play. The operation attempted by Israel to cleanse the Bedouins in the Naqab, the Prawer Plan, was thwarted not by BDS pressure but by the very clear message the Bedouin community sent to the Israeli government of the possible dire consequences of the attempt to forcefully remove a community which had serving members in the army, the police, and on its margins connections to the arsenal of the criminal world—in short there were loads of weapons around.

In a new developing case regarding the attempt of the Israeli government to cleanse the Palestinians from the old city of Akka (Acre), the only effective means will be a strong international campaign spearheaded by a cultural boycott. Here the connection between the racist ideology of Zionism and the actual policies on the ground is part of the tasks of a concrete BDS campaign.

The ability to take this case by case, and the Israeli government is providing us with many of them recently, is crucial. We need to make sure we do not stay at the level of slogans. You know what you are talking about and are very concrete about the kind of atrocities that you are facing. In most cases, you can leave it to an academic debate later on to explain the general context. But as an activist there has to be a direct address to the community of suffering, even if you do not have national leadership and even if the reality is fragmented.

NC: I think that's correct and in this respect I think the South African anti-apartheid movement was a pretty good model. They tended to be pretty concrete. Let's oppose allowing sports teams to participate in international events because of their racist conditions. Let's oppose racist hiring in universities. All of that makes sense. It's directed against particular policies and it's clear what the general background is. It's also intelligible to the audience at home. But there was another aspect of the South African solidarity movement which is very critical. By the 1990s the apartheid regime had virtually no international support. Only two countries—the USA and Britain. They supported apartheid strongly right to the end, particularly Reagan. That was sufficient for the regime, as long as they had US support they did not care, like Israel right now.

That meant that a crucial part of activism had to be directed against the USA, and secondly Great Britain. That's very critical. It's critical now too. Part of the intellectual weakness of the BDS movement is that it is directed against Israel but not against the USA. US policies are absolutely critical. Israel understands, like South Africa at the time, that they can be a pariah state, the whole world can be against them, but that it does not make a difference as long as the USA backs them. That was true in South Africa and it's true in Israel. The US solidarity movement has to focus on that. What are we going to do to change US policies? That is quite critical.

IP: Although of course there are elements of US policy and Israeli policy that are not easily distinguishable.

NC: That's part of the problem. The USA supports Israel not out of benevolence, but because it's useful for US policies. So yes, they do overlap a lot. Also cultural relations, Christian Zionism for example, is part of the demographic base of the Republican Party—extremely anti-Semitic, but pro-Israel. All these things have to be addressed.

IP: I also meant the industrial complex. The academic complex. It's not very autonomous in Israel. It's part of the American milieu in many ways.

NC: Not autonomous, you're right. Such that Israel's major military industry, Rafael, moved their management headquarters to Washington, because that's where the money is.

IP: Sometimes you target Israelis elites and you condemn them for their complacency or their direct involvement in the atrocities. You are also in a way, targeting the octopus that is America, in this respect.

NC: If you make it clear. Not if you do not talk about it.

IP: I agree, you have to clarify. That's a good point.

FB: Can pressure from the bottom up, from civil society, through the boycott movement and other tactics, change US policies?

NC: I think that US foreign policy as in every other case will have to change because of pressure from the bottom. Take South Africa. It was popular pressure which finally induced Congress and even businesses to begin to pull out of South Africa. It could not get to the executive. Reagan vetoed congressional sanctions, but there was enough popular pressure for Congress to override the vetoes. Reagan had then to violate the congressional legislation. Popular pressure did make a difference. That's the same on every other issue. Civil rights, women rights, whatever it may be. That's what has to be done here too. Now, does BDS contribute to that? It could. In fact, it has not much, it might have even been harmful, the way it has been conducted, but it could. If there is groundwork laid by educational programs among the public which makes these actions understandable, helps explain what's happening, and if you can work it out, is directed specifically toward the USA. So for example, the Jordan Valley. I do not think this has been done in the US, it should be. Boycotting products of the Jordan Valley. First of all it harms the Jordan Valley settlement project, but much more significantly, it brings out here that the USA and Israel have a policy of depopulating the Jordan Valley, which is a real ethnic cleansing. Kicking the Palestinians out, whose population is now down to sixty thousand, compared to a couple of hundred thousands in 1967. There is a systematic policy of displacing them, replacing them by Jewish settlements, which leads the way to a form of annexation which would completely imprison any Palestinian entity that might arise somehow—in 30 percent of the West Bank. The US is backing these actions and policies. Something simple like boycotting products is an entry point to bringing out all of these issues. Among the general public that's intelligible. In fact it's already been pretty successful. One of the major successes, to a large extent thanks to young Palestinian activists, has been in the colleges. The atmosphere in the universities around these issues has radically changed. Not many years ago, if I was talking even here, at MIT, on Israel/Palestine, I would have had to have police protection. Now it's totally different. If we were to give a talk tomorrow, we would get a huge audience, engaged, you could not get a hostile question. That's an enormous change, and that can be extended.

Activism among young people has sparked broader popular movements. It's true for the civil rights movement, the antiwar movement. That can have a large effect and it's a matter of considerable concern for the Zionist organizations. They are talking about it, writing about it, they are worried about it. They realize that they are losing the youth. That's going to affect the population. Pretty much like in other cases. It can make a big difference. It tends to be played down in elite discussions. But if you look closely, even in the documentary record, you can see the effect. Take Vietnam again. One of the most interesting parts of the Pentagon Papers, which is never discussed because it is too inflammatory, is at the very end. The Pentagon Papers end in mid-1968, right after the Tet offensive, a big uprising in South Vietnam, which goes on for a couple of months. The president wanted to send more troops after the Tet offensive; the joint chiefs of staff were opposed. They said that they were going to need those troops for civil disorder control in the USA. [They said] "There will be uprisings among young people, women, students, minorities, we are just going to have to suppress them, we cannot send more troops," and they did not. That's not insignificant. It's because of mass popular activism. If that can be done in the Palestine case, I think it can change US policy. Which is not graven in stone. There are a lot of factors that can of course impel it, but they are pretty thin if you look at them. For example, if the significant domestic lobbies in the USA, the business lobbies, which just overwhelm everything else, if they came to the opinion that US policy in support of Israel is harmful to their interests, they would change it very quickly. That can be done.

IP: I think we are talking about two levels of activism here. First the level of more organized activism on the ground such as the BDS movements and the Israeli Apartheid Week projects on campuses that started in Canada in 2005. They were, in a way, narratives created, invented, by young people because there was no guidance from the PLO, no clear leadership that told people how they would like the civil society to act on their behalf. The South Africa and antiwar movements inspired people. What they do, as Noam rightly says and I think it is a great success, is to change the language on campuses, on universities. Things that were taboos are now totally acceptable: it is far more embarrassing to be a pro-Israeli activist today than it was twenty years ago! It is a great success that does not necessarily translate immediately into a change of American policy on the ground, but it is part of a larger process.

The second level of activism is an internal recognition of the complex nature of its possible effect. There is no clear vision or way of assessing the impact activism had in the few cases in recent history which ended long chapters of human abuse. Take for example South Africa. It is difficult to measure the impact of activism, and even the efforts of the liberation movement on the ground that the impact of the fall of the Soviet Union played in toppling the apartheid regime. It is hard to conjure what will be the equivalent historical event in the case of Israel, but that event has to be a catalytic one, whether it is the fall of Saudi Arabia or something else. Whatever it is going to be we should not bother guessing the future. The relevant question is while one waits for the fundamental change in American policy, can one win small battles vis-à-vis its policies? Are there loopholes that would enable activism to convince the American policy makers to condemn or even stop isolated atrocious cases such as preventing the continued ethnic cleansing of Palestinians from the Naqab, Acre, or the Greater Jerusalem area?

Targets probably have to be "modest" in comparison to the big picture, although there is nothing modest in trying to prevent the continued starvation of the Gaza Strip. I am optimistic and I do believe a catalytic event will occur that would fundamentally change the picture. In the meantime, I totally identify with what Noam said about the suffering of the people on the ground and you know it as much as I do, Frank, when you come to the Jordan Valley, and I was just there a week ago, how difficult it is to lift spirits there by telling how impressive has been the shift in Western and American public opinion. This does not alleviate their suffering in any way. You rightly receive stale looks when you tell them enthusiastically about the BDS campaign. They still are denied access to their water and land and are facing the danger of an imminent expulsion.

NC: Yes.

IP: I think expectations on the ground are far more concrete and immediate. Can the solidarity movement outside persuade the American consul in East Jerusalem to come and see with his own eyes what they are subjected to by the Israeli occupation? We need to strike the right balance between our success in changing the conversation in the West—through the actions of the BDS and the Apartheid Week initiatives—and achieving some old activist-style tangible results on the ground.

NC: Yes.

IP: The sense for the need for tangible results is particularly acute when you talk to people in the Gaza Strip.

NC: That can be done by activism here. There could be campaigns here that would get people to pressure the American consul to go to the West Bank. It was actually done in the South African case. I do not want to go too far off on South Africa, but there is a crucial aspect of the end of apartheid that is totally suppressed here and in Britain for reasons of ideological fanaticism. Apartheid was substantially ended by Cuba. The scholarly record on this by now is just overwhelming. The Cubans sent military forces, mostly Black soldiers, who drove the South Africans out of Angola, forced them to leave Namibia, broke the mythology of this white superman, which had a big effect on white and Black South Africa. And the South Africans know it. When Mandela was let out of jail, his first comment was to praise Cubans for their inspiration and their help, because they played a huge part in ending apartheid. You cannot say that in the USA or in England, because we have a kind of religious fanaticism that says that we are not allowed to tell the truth about these matters. But that was an overwhelming factor, and of course, it's missing here. We should think about other models, but it is important to break through the ideological constraints in the West which prevent recognition of what in fact happened. That's pretty important.

IP: There was a beginning of this model although it has not matured in a similar way. In the early days of what was called the Arab Spring, I remember the Israeli bewilderment at seeing young secular Egyptians who manifested and believed in everything the Israelis at least allegedly believed in as well—whether it is liberalism, democracy, and so on—and yet were very clear about Palestine, including in the signs that they were carrying. This combination of highly committed young Arabs to both the idea of Palestine and democracy frightened the Israelis who would be much more comfortable if the pro-Palestinian sentiment were packaged in an anti-democratic way.

NC: Israel's mythology is the villa in the jungle, and then it turns out the jungle was watching the villa!

IP: I am a historian, I am not impressed by a few years and I think we should be very careful when saying that we know exactly where the Arab Spring is going, but it has a potential, a kind of out-of-the-box factor that has not been there before. The unknown factors and actors disable us from predicting too well the future trends. We are familiar with the Arab regimes, the Islamic opposition, and Western policies. But the balance between them can all be reshuffled by the appearance of a new force.

NC: At the moment, things are kind of in limbo, but in the early stages of the Arab Spring there was a very significant solidarity developing between American, European, and Egyptian activists. The Arab Spring began around the time of the Wisconsin uprising. There were messages of support from Egyptian labor leaders to Wisconsin activists, and conversely, Occupy people went to Egypt.

Another aspect of the Arab Spring which cannot be discussed in the USA for ideological reasons is the role of labor. The militant labor movement was very significant. One of the lasting achievements is a substantial boost in the opportunities for labor organizing which had been crushed under the previous regime. Again, that's the kind of topic that you are not supposed to talk about here, but it's important.

FB: What do you make of the American Studies Association passing a resolution endorsing an academic boycott of Israel? How important do you think that is?

NC: Well, that's what I had in mind when I was bringing up the Jenin fiasco. It's very much like it. It was not prepared; it was guaranteed to create a backlash that would overwhelm it. It was not thought out properly. The result is that there has been a shift from concern with Israeli crimes and US support for them to the issue of academic freedom. Very much like what happened in 2002. Shift from focus on Jenin and the crimes there, and the US background, to a discussion about anti-Semitism at Harvard. The net effect of the ASA resolution, predictably, has been a huge discussion in the USA about academic freedom. That's harmful to the Palestinians. You have to think these things through. What is the effect going to be of the resolution that you are putting forth if you have not created an understanding among the population you are trying to reach? An understanding about what the significance of this is. It's going to be harmful. So anybody who looks at the resolution will ask immediate questions. The resolution began, "Whereas the USA supports Israeli crimes, therefore let's boycott Tel Aviv University." That's not what is supposed to follow. It should say, "Whereas the USA supports Israeli crimes, let's boycott Harvard." Well that's not a good proposal either, but at least it would be logical. I think around a hundred university presidents already immediately issued condemnations and there is a big debate around academic freedom. What good does it do to the Palestinians? It diverts attention away from the issue. And of course it does not affect Israel in any way at all. I would contrast that to the boycott of the products of the Jordan Valley. That's significant. First of all it has an impact and secondly people can understand it. It can be an entry wedge toward bringing out the major issues. Like what Israel is doing in the Jordan Valley altogether. How come they are able to get away with it? Only because of US support. That opens opportunities that have all the right characteristics. It harms the Israeli government policies significantly and it also opens the way to creating the kind of popular understanding and activism in the US that can change policy. On the other hand the ASA resolution had the opposite effect.

IP: Here, I don't entirely agree with Noam. I am now spending a sabbatical year in Israel and I see on the ground the reactions to the ASA and similar kinds of declarations. I do think it has some positive effects in Israel. For instance it takes the intellectual academic elite of Israel out of its comfort zone. They are worried. They may not read the declaration pedantically, but they understand that what they are seeing, as far as they are concerned, is a kind of a domino effect by which societies of American academics are going to find ways or look for better or more efficient ways to convey a message to them that they are unhappy with the Israeli academic basic position on Israeli policies and so on.

There is also very little danger for backlash from Israel in the sense that the present political and cultural elites in Israel are so entrenched in their fanatic positions that they cannot dig deeper or become more intransigent than they are today. As for the liberal Zionist elements within these elites, I think campaigns like this embarrass them in a positive way. It forces them to adopt clearer positions on the oppression and occupation. They are being reminded in a very forceful way that their self-image of Israel as a democratic society is questioned by people they respect and societies and associations to which they want to belong. That is the way of sending a wake-up call to them.

Secondly, although there is a backlash on the part of the American presidents of universities and so on, I do think it comes to the issue of democratization in the academic system. In a similar way you could say that a civil society action against Israel will not be endorsed by Capitol Hill, in fact they might go and do the opposite: declare a counter position. I know it is not a democratic system; it is not supposed to be. It is a production of knowledge system, but it is also a human organism which has two kinds of memberships: members who are running the system and members who are part of the system. The latter are the ones who have a view about Israel; they have other ways of expressing it, they are also using academic societies for that purpose. The fact that this is not reflected in the positions of the heads of universities is not necessarily a bad thing. It is a kind of tough conversation that we are having with each other in modern academia.

NC: I mentioned the hundred university presidents, but it's the academic world. For example, if you read the *Chronicle of Higher Education*, there are articles critical of the ASA resolution by longterm militant activists. People like Linda Gordon and others who have been at the forefront of activism in all kind of issues. They are the kind of people who are critical of the resolution. Now there could have been a sensible resolution. If the resolution had said, let's boycott in some fashion Bar-Ilan, because of the Ariel campus, in the middle of the West Bank, that would have been comparable to the Jordan Valley boycott. It is understandable, it makes good sense, they are directly involved in the occupation as an academic institution and it also brings out the basic fact about what the occupation is doing. Why is there an Ariel campus? It splits the West Bank in two, maybe in five by now. All of that is important to bring out. When you say let's carry out these actions against Israeli institutions, why not against US institutions, which have a much worse record? I mean, it's not just the university presidents. The ASA resolution is not going to affect construction workers. It reaches the academic world. And in the academic world it shifted attention from Israeli crimes, and crucially US support for them, to the general question about academic freedom. In that respect it's rather like what happened in the Jenin case. I think those things have to be thought through carefully. Israeli institutions are not more blameworthy than American institutions, much less. Focusing on Bar-Ilan or any others directly involved in the occupation could have been much more effective.

IP: The Hebrew University is expanding on the land of Issawiya.

NC: Then that should be brought up, that would make sense.

IP: I agree with Noam that it would be good to have a thorough study on this.* We still don't have a clear study that tells ordinary people in the United States why the Israeli academia should be targeted. There is a need to present a clear proof to people about their complacency: the level of their collaboration with the occupation and the oppression.

Although BDS was an initiative of the Palestinian civil society, it emerged parallel to similar initiatives in the West by pro-Palestinian activists. They were looking for ways of sending messages to Israel, to show that enough is enough. If you are an academic or a trade union activist, you use your peer group and you say, we have to do something as academics, journalists, artists, filmmakers. You also have to know better what are you targeting and why you are targeting it. In this, I don't see as much harm as Noam does, but I do agree that, as I said before, a more concrete and transparent action is needed: you explain to people why you are doing what you are doing and do not leave it on this general level which says everybody's a criminal and so on and therefore by association should be targeted. I think there could be a constructive criticism rather than killing the impulse.

---

* A study by the Alternative Information Center from 2009, "Academic Boycott of Israel," can be found online.

This is a very successful impulse. When you view it on the ground in Israel you can sense the apprehension that the next step would be, as suggested by Jibril Rajub, to take Israel out of the world or European football association. There you hear clearly that Israeli sports people know that the only reason that may happen is the way their state is treating the Palestinians in general and Palestinian footballers in particular. No discourse on anti-Semitism is heard in this context.

NC: That would be like the South African case. It picks out actions that are unacceptable on the part of the state and intelligible on the part of the audience you are trying to reach. The ASA was the opposite.

FB: I agree that thorough studies on the implications of Israeli institutions in the occupation and Israeli crimes need to be done . . .

NC: For some of it it's kind of obvious—the Ariel campus, you hardly have to study it.

IP: The more general one is more difficult to understand.

NC: The Hebrew University one will take work.

FB: . . . still, from what I understand, and from what I have read, it looks like most of them are indeed complicit in the occupation and in Israeli crimes. So even though I agree that more studies will be useful and are important, I do think that the educational process is happening during and after a resolution like the ASA one is passed. The debate in the US is on academic freedom, but people are also asking questions like why is the ASA, a respected institution, asking to boycott Israel? This question might not have been raised if the resolution had not been passed.

IP: I think what Noam is trying to say, if I understood correctly, at least this is what I think, is that it is the other way around. You have not yet won the argument that Israel, as a political entity, is problematic. You have won the argument that Israel should not occupy the West Bank and the Gaza Strip, but that is something else. If the whole boycott movement were focused on getting the Israeli army out of the West Bank and the Gaza Strip, I think there would have been less argument about it. As you know, I support it and I think there is a problem with the state of Israel as it is, not just with what it is doing in the West Bank but also what it is doing in Haifa, in the Naqab, and in Acre. This is not yet clear to many people in the West. I think that people there are not aware that they are facing a bigger injustice than just the Israeli policies in the West Bank and the Gaza Strip. BDS so far has been an impulse, not a strategy. I think it is an impulse that needs to be accompanied by more thorough analysis, study, and explanation.

NC: I would only add to that that critically the USA has to be brought into it.

IP: Yes, I agree.

NC: It's the crucial support for Israeli actions. Very much like in the South African case, where it was the US that maintained apartheid until the end.

FB: How would you bring the US more to the front? It seems to me like people do know, right now, that the US is complicit in Israel's crimes. How would you even start boycotting the USA?

NC: Take, say, the negotiations, that are going on. The solidarity movement ought to be focused on that. Negotiations which are organized by the USA, which is a participant in the conflict.

That makes about as much sense as if Iran was called upon to mediate the Shia/Sunni conflict in Iraq. People would just laugh. The very fact that the US is organizing it should be viewed as a joke. That's not understood. It should be understood. It's not just three billion dollars in military aid, it's also the vetoes, and the ideological support. That's crucial support in the USA. The striking case in the USA is the way the Cuban role in South Africa has been suppressed. To this day, you read articles by scholars that are suppressing it. These are things you have to deal with.

CHAPTER FOUR

The Future

FB: Is an Israeli Spring possible?

NC: For the last ten years especially, there has been a very strong shift in Israeli mentality and politics toward the right, nationalism, toward more extremism, there is a kind of circling the wagons mentality which was also true in South Africa toward the end. "The world hates us because they are all anti-Semitic so we will do what we want." Nothing is their fault; everything is somebody else's fault, a lot of brutality. I mean sometimes, unbelievable. The scenes for example during Cast Lead, the brutal attack on Gaza with Israelis sitting on beach chairs on the hills, applauding every time a bomb fell. This is beyond obscenity. But unfortunately, it is a large part of the population. There are countertendencies, but they are, as far as I can see, pretty limited. When there was the Rothschild demonstration, the tent city, kind of Occupy-type thing—except if you look at it, it is pretty narrow: it is, "I want something better for me,

This conversation between Noam Chomsky, Ilan Pappé, and Frank Barat was recorded on January 17, 2014, and has been condensed and edited.

I want to be able to get an apartment." In fact, there was a decision
by the organizers that they could not mention the Palestinians, so it
is just: "What can I get to make my life a little better?" It is true that
Israeli society has been shifting from what used to be a kind of more
or less Scandinavian-style social democracy to a kind of an extreme
version of neoliberal, kind of a caricature of neo-liberalism, pretty
much like the US, with sharp inequalities, wealth, and privileges.
There is a strong effort to have an appeal to Western youth and
youth culture and so on with the secular mood of Tel Aviv. In Tel
Aviv, we have gay bars and things like that—it may be the gay center of the Mediterranean.

I think is it becoming an ugly and kind of suicidal society. They
are very concerned about what they call delegitimation and that is
true they are delegitimizing themselves. It is a choice I think I may
have mentioned that before, my own feeling is that this is virtually
inevitable since 1971 when they basically made the decision to re-
ject security in favor of expansion, and then lots of things followed
more or less not automatically but fairly predictably and they've
been happening. There are slight changes, how significant they will
be I don't know, in the repression of the Palestinian population. For
example the most extreme racist laws in Israel are those concerning
the land. About 92 percent of the land was in the hands of Keren
Kayemet, the Jewish National Fund, which is an organization that
had contracts with the state of Israel that required them to work
only for the benefit of "people of Jewish race/religion and origin"
(that was the phrase) that with the whole array of administrative
arrangements, bureaucratic structures meant that in effect they
control over 90 percent of the land—which meant that it was Arab-
free basically. There is a crack in that structure, about ten years ago,

I think it was in 2000, the Supreme Court did invalidate it in principle with regard to a particular settlement. They said they could not keep Arabs out and I think after five or six years the Arab couple who was trying to live there were finally allowed in but, Ilan, you would know better than I do, I do not think it had any noticeable effects anywhere else and now legislation in the Parliament is trying to undercut it. It is one example of policies that are pretty rigid. There are some things that are going on that really shock me. I learned recently from Ruchama Marton, a wonderful woman who is the head of the Israeli Physicians for Human Rights organization, and you probably know this, that in Israeli hospitals, in maternity wards, Palestinian women citizens have to go to different wards than the Jewish women. . . . Things like that go on all the time.

I don't think it is a very pretty picture; you can't separate Israel itself from Greater Israel with their planning which is being implemented in the West Bank. People forget about the Golan Heights, but that is illegally occupied in violation of explicit Security Council orders. The world likes to forget that is Syria basically, and of course Gaza remains a horrible prison, brutalized, now it is even worse because of the Egyptian military regime which is closing off the tunnels and threatening to punish Gaza. The whole picture is extremely unpleasant to use a very mild, understated word and I suspect it will get worse.

IP: Yes, I fully agree. I think it is an important question that you pose because for anyone who is watching from the outside, who is an activist, who is interested in analyses of a possible change from within the answer to this question will dictate one's strategy in the future. If you come to the conclusion which I think was at the heart of the strategy against apartheid in South Africa that change from within is not imminent, it is not going to take place, of course then the pressure from the outside becomes the major hope for change or military defeat which was an option during the age of the liberation movements but is probably less relevant today.

In this connection it might be helpful to mention two other related issues or rather two disappearances. One is the disappearance of liberal Zionism as a significant actor on the Israeli political stage. There seems to be no room in Israel for those who try to square a universalist point of view, be it liberal or socialist, with the racist definition of Zionism.

The second issue is the disappearance of the Green Line after forty-five years of occupation and with it has gone the distinction between what is "here" and what is "there." The most recent indications for this is the creeping annexation of Area C by the Israelis and the suggestion of the Israeli foreign minister Avigdor Liberman to annex the Palestinian citizens of Israel in Wadi Ara to the West Bank. This brought to the fore more clearly the Israeli ethnic policies of dispossession and occupation and showed that these policies were not limited to a certain area or one group of Palestinians.

These two additional developments accentuate the conviction that we should not expect a change from within Israel. There are few movements that try to challenge it from within, there is even a younger generation that is trying to do things that have not been done before like the Anarchists Against the Wall, New Profile, and the like; but they are very small in numbers and they do not expand at any pace that would make you optimistic that they represent a more massive movement.

It may also be useful to mention in this context the 2011 Israeli social justice protests. It shows changes in the agenda of the Israeli middle class, but alas they are still not connected in any visible way to conflict with the Palestinians. One of the main reasons that until 2011 it fared much better than in most Western countries, even after the 2008 financial crisis, was the way the overdraft banking system worked in Israel. Regardless of your salary, you had a license to spend from the bank. It meant that a member of the middle class could live well beyond their means and their actual salaries. This fiesta has now come to an end and the bitter reality has unfolded: the average middle-class salary does not allow for a decent standard of living and in particular decent housing. This realization was the main impetus behind the 2011 protests. The banks have stopped doing this, overdrafts, and Israelis had to start to live according to the not-so-high salaries and they could not afford what is the most expensive item in the market, accommodation, and that was the major motive for the protest movement.

What it means in macroeconomic terms is that the middle class is dragged down and the rich become richer. In the long run it can have impact on the questions we discuss. A society without socio-economic integrity and solidarity can collapse from within, and not even a strong ideological indoctrination would keep it intact.

NC: In comparison to South Africa, there really are differences in this regard. In South Africa, the oppressed population, the Black population, was 85 percent of the total population. They were their entire workforce, they depended on them. Also there was a huge Cuban force driving South Africa out of its neighboring countries that it was trying to integrate. Apart from that, there was in the 1980s, and after Soweto in 1987, a very fierce militant Black activism from within. There is nothing comparable in either of those two things in Israel.

IP: No, not really.

FB: Let's come to Palestinian society and Palestinian politics. Haidar Eid, a professor in Gaza, recently wrote for Al-Shabaka *that "the only way forward may be to dis-participate in the current Palestinian political system, there is no space for radical change in the current system and that Palestinians should rebuild from the bottom up, organically a real political alternative."*

Do you agree with this idea of dis-participation and then should not we apply this idea to Europe and the West too? Our governments being Democrats, Republicans, the Left, the Right do not represent us and this idea of dis-participating from the current system might be a way forward to rebuild something much better?

NC: Saying this for someone who is actually living in Gaza, like a cry of desperation, is pretty understandable. As I said, I was there recently, the situation is very harsh, but what does it mean? I mean what do you dis-participate from?

In the West, I don't think it means much either, it is true our governments do not represent us, but there is plenty that can be done about that—we don't live in fascist states. There are lots of opportunities. State power is there, but its capacity to repress is not really great. It is a pretty fragile structure and it can be influenced and affected. Separating yourself from it, I don't know what that means . . . does that mean going to Montana, getting a plot of land, and raising your own food? There are interpretations of that notion which make some sense like localism in agriculture, developing local production, urban agriculture, a lot of things that can be done that kind of extricate people from the dominant social economic forces, but there are plenty of opportunities within the existing framework, within institutions, for major changes that do not exist in Gaza. I don't really think these are comparable notions.

IP: It is important in this context to pay attention to the sentiment on the ground and mainly the wish to rely less on existing political structures as they have highly disappointed the Palestinians wherever they are.

If we want to respond to this sentiment, we can cautiously at least say we are looking for new thinking on how to reframe the relationship between Jews and Arabs between the River Jordan and the Mediterranean. But this should not be done against the existing structures but in conversation with them. Engaging as many people as possible in new thinking can be very helpful whether they are from the Fatah, Hamas, or Israeli political parties—a good departure point to agree on how to analyze or depict the present reality. If these structures are not relevant to that new reality, they will disappear anyway, I do not have to declare the need to dismantle them.

I will give a few examples: Israelis can either deny the fact that they live with the West Bank longer than they lived without it and therefore territorially this is the space (Israel and the West Bank, as well as the Gaza Strip) in which they have to find a solution—not just in the West Bank. Palestinians can deny that there is already a third generation of Zionist settlers on the ground, but they will have to accept that they missed the historical opportunity, if ever there was one, to get rid of the first wave of invaders.

There are also two different tasks ahead: the Israeli wish to keep the status quo and the Palestinian crave to change it. The former have a lot to lose in terms of privileges and power, the latter everything to gain. Thus the need to pressure the former is the key for peace or reconciliation.

Maybe another way forward is the one Noam hinted at. Somehow finding a way of convincing the Israelis they are heading on a suicidal track. And add to this showing their own responsibility for that state of affairs. They are building walls, arming themselves to death, and yet their insecurity is growing. This is where one should look for a way of not giving up the utopian ideal of a non-state future and the need to find a political structure that as soon as possible would bring an ending to the suffering on the ground.

NC: I suspect that there is a not-too-hidden sense among the Israelis of the fragility of their future. One indication is that there are a number of people who are trying to get a double passport.

IP: Absolutely.

NC: I don't know what the proportion is, but it is large.

IP: True, it is a lot.

NC: Worse come to worst they will come to New York . . .

IP: Not the Arab Jews . . . they've got nowhere to go!

NC: I read somewhere that the most rapidly growing Jewish community in the World is in Berlin . . .

IP: Yes, it is absolutely true. It is a bit ironic!

NC: I think we have to ask ourselves what Israel is planning and will be able to implement as long as the US supports it and ask ourselves how do we react to that not-too-distant future. What you said about Area C and Wadi Ara I think is right to the point here. It seems that what they are clearly planning is Greater Israel, which will of course include the Golan Heights, and will separate Gaza from the West Bank, which is a crucial violation of Oslo and everything else, but they don't care about laws. As far as the West Bank is concerned, they have certainly planned to take over everything within what is called the "Separation Wall," the annexation wall. Greater Jerusalem is maybe five times greater than what it ever was in history and systematically kicks Palestinians out—there are practically no Palestinians institutions left. Then come these corridors, to the east of Greater Jerusalem one goes through the town of Maale Adumim, which was built primarily in the 1990s, just as a way of bisecting the West Bank. The lands of Maale Adumim go way beyond the settlement; they practically reach Jericho, which bisects the West Bank. They haven't yet succeeded in filling in one area that is called E1.

So far, every American president has blocked that pre-Obama. He has said nothing about it except that it wasn't helpful, so they may be able to fill out that encirclement of Greater Jerusalem. These corridors are to the north, one going to Ariel which we talked about, one to Kedumin that would cut through much of the rest of the area. It looks as if they were planning to take over Area C and they deny it, but there have been large parts later that have been taken over. The Jordan Valley, which Israel claims it occupies only because of security, is now in fact inaccessible to most Palestinians since Israel has used the "security" issue to build more and more settlements. Looking at the plans that are being implemented, there are definite intentions to take over the Jordan Valley. It will mean that this Greater Israel, if it looks something like this, will have a very few Palestinians in it. They won't have what is called the demographic problem, too many non-Jews in the Jewish state, a horrible concept . . . but they won't really have it and in fact if it becomes integrated into Israel, as I am sure they've planned, it will actually decrease the proportion of Palestinians. Now, they have got to do some hand-wringing about land swap and I suspect it will be just like you said where this is happening in the northern Galilee [with] a very heavily Arab population. The population apparently doesn't want it, not because they love Israel, but because they don't want to go from being forced out of a wealthy, first-world developed society into what one of them recently called a "punching bag" in an article on *Haaretz*, which is what Palestine is turning out to be. A racist society will force them out even if they don't want to leave. It will be presented to the West as a very gracious act of letting the Palestinian state have a piece of Israel, the piece that we don't want because there are too many Arabs there and maybe, you know, giving them a little bit of land in the Negev. That looks like the picture on the ground, and if so, that is the picture we have to face.

FB: Following up on this and talking about a new reality, for you Professor Pappé, the new reality is already one regime, one political system governing both Palestinians and Israeli Jews, a common state reality, you are urging us to advocate and fight to change the nature of the system, the rules, the internal laws, et cetera. Professor Chomsky, you've been an advocate and you've written about a common state, one state, a binational state for decades, do we need to go through two states because of the consensus to eventually get to one state?

NC: Yes, that is because the way I see it, Israel and the United States do not want one state and will never accept it. They have a preferable alternative from their point of view to take over what I've just described, this Greater Israel which is not going to have many Palestinians in it—in fact, a smaller percentage than in Israel today. The big Palestinian concentrations are going to be outside, population concentrations will be outside. The plan for them is I think they can mostly rot, or maybe flee. There will be a standard neocolonial structure in which there is a center for the elite. So you go to Ramallah, nice houses, theaters, bars where Westerners can come and see how lovely Palestine is, which you find in every Third World country, the poorest country you want in Central Africa and you can find these sectors there that are for the elite which look like Paris or London. In fact, if you go back to the 1990s, Israeli industrialists openly and literally urged the government to shift from what they called a colonial program to a neocolonial program, which means establish this Third World–style entity with most of them rotting but with some kind of a center for rich Palestinians, the privileged ones, the elite, and so on. If that is correct, then there are really two options. One is, either this, which will have very few Palestinians, they will be somewhere else and the other one is two states. Two states is a rotten solution, but at least it has the merit of having overwhelming international support that has been blocked by the United States for thirty-five years now but has overwhelming international support. I don't feel myself that the settlements are irreversible.

I'd be interested in Ilan's opinion, but my feeling is that Israel could do what it could have done if they wanted to in Gaza. They did not have to force the people out of Gaza and that was a game that they played to impress the West. They could have said, on August 1, "The IDF (Israeli Defense Forces) is going to leave Gaza, you climb into the lorries we are giving you, we will take you from your subsidized homes in Gaza to nicer subsidized homes in the West Bank." Then they could do the same thing for the West Bank. Say the IDF is pulling out, there you can go and a lot of people in the West Bank reckon that it is a nice place to live and they have subsidized towns, pleasant suburbs, Tel Aviv and Jerusalem.

They've got superhighways taking them right into Tel Aviv without seeing any Arabs and so on. If some people want to hang on to every rock I don't see why they should not be allowed to do it, they can be in a Palestinian state. That is a conceivable possibility. I think the chances are not very high—in fact, pretty low—but that seems to me the only realistic alternative to this Greater Israel picture.

Now, if some kind of two-state settlement, no matter how rotten it is, is established, my guess is that the borders are going to erode, because if you know the country at all, there is no way to draw a line, it would not make sense whatsoever. In fact, when there have been relaxations of tension in the past, there has been some erosion of the sharp boundaries, and commercial, cultural, and other kinds of interchange began to take place. We don't know where it could lead, but it could lead to closer integration, you know a kind of longer term that we are all talking about, thinking about some sort of a federal integrated society. As I said earlier, I don't worship the imperial borders, I don't think they have to be maintained either, but I just don't see any other alternatives to those two alternatives.

Talking about one state is kind of interesting to keep at the back of your mind, but it is just not one of the options. I think, these are the two options and I think it is misleading from people on every side, the Shin Bet, Palestinian leaders, international commentators to talk as if the choices are either two states or one state. Those are simply not the choices. The choices are Greater Israel or two states and Greater Israel doesn't have Palestinians or a few Palestinians.

IP: I see it a bit differently. I think that the balance of power on the ground and the kind of relationship Israel has with the United States and the international community ensures that the alternative of two states will always be implemented more or less the way Israel understands the two-state solution.

This version actually means the creation of a Greater Israel. Despite the international support for allegedly two distinct states the end result will not be two very different models. They would be different in the sense of international legitimacy and in the two-state solution the Palestinians will enjoy some symbolic independence and could display some insignia, but the basic relationship between the Israelis and the Palestinians would not change.

I do not see much logic in supporting something that would actually legitimize the Greater Israel option. The two-state solution in 2014 can only go one way—toward the international legitimization of the two-state solution. The international community is looking for someone like Abu Mazen to accept an Israeli notion of a two-state solution that it purports and this, if successful, can perpetuate a Greater Israel through international legitimacy.

Against the already existing Greater Israel one has to conduct a campaign of regime change based on human and civil rights equality and hope the regional and international developments would help it to mature. What the international community is doing right now reminds us once more of the famous Jewish joke of someone looking for a key he lost where there was light but not where he lost the key.

NC: We may have a slightly different expectation of what might happen, I don't think anybody can know, but I think we ought to be able to agree on this. The standard discourse is highly misleading; there is no choice between two states and one state, that is not a choice and again this standard discourse is on all sides, you hear it from the Israeli leadership and the Palestinian leadership. I was surprised by what Ian Lustick wrote,* but this is almost universal, there is no one-state option. What's left is two possibilities, either the one option of Greater Israel or some other version of it which will be called two states or maybe something like the international consensus. The question is what are the probabilities that the international consensus or something like it can be realized, not just the Israeli version of it?

About that, I don't think we know. My feeling is, you might be right, maybe it's water under the bridge, but it is also possible that this still remains a live option, exactly what it would be like, maybe something like the Geneva proposals, which were not wonderful, but they are not the Greater Israel version. If this could be possible, it would be different from Greater Israel. For one thing, the Jordan Valley would not be included, same for most of Area C, and it would include some kind of shrinking division of Jerusalem, with Palestinian institutions there and it would not be land swaps with Wadi Ara but maybe with fertile land near Gaza which could give Gaza some opportunities. Those are not huge differences, but I think they are differences and how realistic that is I don't know . . . my own feeling is that if US policies shifted it would be realistic.

Again, I don't think we can push the South Africa analogy too far because at this point there are too many differences like the huge internal Black activism inside South Africa, no possible counterpart to that in Israel, the military defeat of South Africa by Cuba, there is nothing like that . . . but some things are similar like US policy. Europe can also take a position here too. Europe is

---

* See Ian S. Lustick, "Two-State Illusion," op-ed, *New York Times*, September 14, 2013.

pretty timid, it doesn't want to bother or interfere with the bosses' priorities, but they don't have to be like that. Part of the Third World is also becoming more independent, the US is still overwhelmingly powerful, but in the whole world the power is being diffused and it might make a difference. These countries are not enormously powerful, but still things could happen in the Arab world. I don't think the Arab Spring is finished, there are other things that are going to break open and at least such developments might lead to possible realizations of a bad but preferable two-state option. I think this is a matter that we cannot predict.

IP: There are other things we can do. There are two ways of looking at the one-state/two-state dichotomy. One is to say that this is an argument about what is the best solution in the future; the other way of looking at it is a way of describing the reality today. For instance if Palestinians inside Israel support the two-state solution, it means they still accept Arafat's contention during the days of Oslo that they are not part of the equation or the solution. And moreover, that they prefer to participate in the present Israeli system and not follow the agenda of the other Palestinian groups. But if they adopt Haidar Eid's position, that means that even they do not have the political power to change the reality now on the ground they still have the right, as Edward Said put it in 1982, "to narrate" their own version of the past and future.

But of course I have to concede that it is not easy to get a clear picture of the Palestinian attitudes, especially those who live in historical Palestine, on this question. Palestinians living in Israel may want the PLO to represent them but declaring it will be suicidal for them; at the same time they are fully aware of the limitation of their representatives in the Israeli Knesset to cater for their needs.

In between these predicaments, they nonetheless begin to adapt to the new realities. The intensifying cultural, political, social, and economic connections between Palestinians living on both sides of the Green Line, and even with the exilic communities abroad, shows that on a small scale and without broadcasting it, they refer to the reality as one state and also seem to share a vision of it.

From a different angle a similar development is taking place on the Jewish side. The veteran settlers of the West Bank have been there as long as most of the Jews inside Israel. They are either redeemers of an ancient land in their own eyes who want to continue the dispossession of the Palestinians or they are settlers wherever they are who have to come to terms with the local people. What matters is not how many Israelis support the two-state solution—many of them do—but how they regard Greater Jerusalem, Qiryat Arba, and Ariel and the Jordan Valley. The vast majority regards this is a part of a Jewish state in a two-state solution. And in such a scenario nothing is left for the other state and what they mean is a support for a one-state version in which Zionism continues to prevail as a racist ideology or if convinced they would eventually accept a different democratic basis for such a state.

From my perspective, thus, a support of a one-state solution is activism that promotes the whole space as one land and the people as one people. What we should not succumb to is the Zionist version of the two states that limits the idea of a Jewish Palestine with few Palestinians in it to "just" 80 percent of Palestine. I still think the principal motive behind Israelis' support for the two-state solution is not reconciliation with the Palestinians but a wish to control as much of the land with as few Palestinians in it as possible.

NC: It is a different scenario and perspective. Let me go back to your distinction between what can be done in the inside and what can be done on the outside. What I think about the issue, concentrating on the work that can be done on the outside, I can't do anything about what Palestinians will decide and you, quite properly, are asking what can be done from the inside. I think these are kind of complementary. I don't think they have to be conflicting, but from the outside, my perspective, I think the task here and in Europe is to delegitimize the occupation, which is possible, delegitimize Israel insofar as it is involved in the occupation, press forward as much as possible to get the US to drop its unilateral opposition to diplomatic settlement along the lines that were laid out thirty-five years ago and see what the options are to create some alternatives to this Greater Israel picture which we see developing.

IP: But also delegitimize Israel when it mistreats the Palestinians inside Israel.

NC: Yes, we should of course be opposed to internal oppression in every country.

But these are kind of separate things. Like when people talk about apartheid, it is a little bit misleading. I mean, inside Israel, there is repression, but it is not apartheid. In the Occupied Territories, it's much worse than apartheid; Black South Africa was not like the Occupied Territories.

IP: But that is separation. Even the Israelis cannot keep the separation for too long. You can see that the same units that have been used to disperse demonstrations in the West Bank are now used to disperse demonstrations in the Negev. The same laws or rather emergency regulations that were applied only in the West

Bank and the Gaza Strip are now sort of seeping through into Israel because the nature of the relationship is changing.

NC: It is correct, but if Greater Israel does get established, they won't care about what's happening outside it; they may occasionally send the IDF there to smash up Nablus, but it is irrelevant, it is your business, you rot over there, we are going to take care of the things that happen inside with not many Palestinians. I think a thrust of activism is trying to expose that, expose it, not suppress it and it is being suppressed by the one-state/two-state discourse. So, not suppress it, expose it and struggle against it.

IP: On this, I agree.

FB: South Africa got rid of institutionalized or legal apartheid in the nineties, but when you look at South African society today and I think Professor Chomsky, you mentioned that yesterday, it is putting a few Black faces in power and keeping the same system in place. So looking at, let's say, a common state or one state, if it was ever to happen, how do you make sure you do not reproduce the South African experience?

NC: You see, that presupposes that Israel would ever want to take in the Palestinian population in the West Bank and Gaza and I don't think they will. That is the crucial difference from South Africa. South Africa had to incorporate the Black population, they had no choice. First of all, it was the vast majority of the population and secondly, it was their workforce. They could not say, okay we will let you go rot somewhere and then they would disappear, but Israel can, that is the Greater Israel option. There are some people even on the right that would say let's take them all over. But I think what they are going to do is what we've been describing: create this Greater Israel, which won't have a lot of Palestinians and repress them inside [the country], but then the South Africa option doesn't arise. What happened in South Africa, let me say, was a kind of recognition around 1990 by international capital by South African businessmen that were privileged South Africans, by the United States that this cannot go on for reasons that don't exist in the Israel case as we mentioned and therefore they made an agreement which Mandela authorized when he became a freed leader, that they would end formal apartheid and keep the socio-economic structure, which for most Africans did not change a lot. Maybe it's actually worse for them, but that is not going to happen in Israel/Palestine because they do not want the population.

IP: I think, in a bizarre way it is, maybe I am going too far with this, kind of a silver lining and I'll explain what I mean. It is very clear that the South African post-apartheid model cannot work in Israel, in other words, you cannot buy the Israelis by persuading them to give up their racist ideology in return for maintaining their economic privileges. This is not going to work. In a very bizarre way, Israeli apartheid, if we can call it that, or racist ideology, is far more religious and dogmatic than the white supremacist one in South Africa. Although it had its churches and its own version of theocratic and religious justifications, basically it was a matter of keeping the privileges [intact] and once they were secured in the post-apartheid system you win over quite a lot of people among the white population, which is not going to work in Israel. You will not convince the high-tech sector in Israel that they can be as rich as they are now but they have to live in a more democratic system. Why can I say? It is a bit of a silver lining, unless I am totally pessimistic about the ability of the younger generations to come to aspire for a better world; this would be a striking example in the twenty-first century of something deplorable, un-acceptable, because it means you have a segregationist society that is only interested in this core racist ideology and that it is easy to see in such a situation and I think that is why these differences are so important.

NC: I don't know if I am saying something different, but I would stress again that one crucial difference between Israel and South Africa is that Israel is separationist and South Africa was not. South Africa had to incorporate the Black population; Israel wants to get rid of them. They can do this by drawing the lines around this Greater Israel—expelling Palestinians in it. What they are in fact doing and slowly, is step by step constructing this monstrous thing—Greater Israel—that will not have a lot of Palestinians. The compromise you mentioned in South Africa won't be possible.

IP: No, it won't work in Israel.

CHAPTER FIVE

Inside Israel

FB: Ilan, you are a historian, you've published numerous books, among them the famous and controversial for some people Ethnic Cleansing of Palestine *in 2006. In 2007 you moved to England where you are currently teaching history at Exeter University. You are part of what is called by some people "the new historians" who give a new analysis and narrative of the history of Zionism and the history of the creation of Israel. You've taken some radical positions against the state of Israel. Why and when did you decide to stand on the Palestinians' side? And what were the consequences for you, being Israeli?*

IP: Changing one's point of view on such a crucial issue is a long journey, it doesn't happen in one day and it doesn't happen because of one event. I've tried in one of my books called *Out of the Frame* to describe this journey out of Zionism to a critical position against Zionism. If I had to choose a formative event that really changed my point of view in a dramatic way, it would be the Israeli

This conversation between Ilan Pappé, Frank Barat, and Frank's brother Florent Barat was recorded on October 20, 2013, and has been condensed and edited.

attack on Lebanon in 1982. For us who grew up in Israel, it was the first non-consensus war, the first war that obviously was a war of choice: Israel was not attacked, Israel attacked. Then the first Intifada happened. These events were eye-openers in many ways for people like myself who already had some doubts about Zionism, about the historical version we learned at school.

It is a long journey and once you take it, you are facing your own society, you are even facing your own family and it is not a nice position to be in. People who know Israel know that it is an intimate and vibrant society so if you are against it, you feel it in every aspect of your life. I think this is one of the reasons why it takes a bit longer for the people like me to come to the point where you say there is no return: you have to subscribe to these views whatever the repercussions are.

FB: I find what you are saying about Israel very interesting. Most nation-states are very good propagandists, but Israel has taken this to another level. I know someone, whom you also know, Nurit Peled-Elhanan, who has written a book about the way Arabs are portrayed in Israeli schoolbooks to show the world the amount of brainwashing and propaganda in Israel that starts from a very early age. Can you tell us more about this society as you've experienced this yourself as well?

IP: Indeed. It is a very indoctrinated society, probably more than most Western societies and more than the non-Western societies. It is not because of coercion that people are indoctrinated; it is a powerful indoctrination from the moment you are born to the moment you die. The people in power don't expect you to get out of it because you seem to be swimming in this fluid. What Nurit Peled-Elhanan says in her books is that you could compare becoming an anti-Zionist to a religious person becoming an atheist and still believing that maybe God is there and maybe he will punish him and punish you for being sacrilegious and so on. One should think about the way you are brought up to believe that there are some truisms of life that if you challenge them, you need to clean yourself up to the bottom to be sure that you are able to move on because otherwise you have all these doubts all the time. It was so powerful. But I think there is a difference between my generation and the present generation of Nurit's sons and my own sons: they know more than we did because of the Internet and what goes on. I think it is more difficult for the Israelis now to rely just on indoctrination although they are doing a good job. There are a very few among the young people of Israel who challenge Zionism. I hope that the world has become more opened with what happened in the Arab world as well. You thought that these were closed societies who would not know what is going on, so I hope this is going to change, but for us, we were like in a bubble, we did not know that there was a different existence; it was very difficult to get out of it.

FB: I guess the older generation, your generation and Nurit's, the amount of cognitive dissonance as well when you've believed in something so strongly all your life, even though the facts show after a while that you are wrong, it is so hard to accept that you were wrong for, let's say, thirty or forty years of your life. You see that all the time, at events when you always see the same people coming to every single Palestinian event, I always think, they know as much as I do about Palestine and they know the facts. How come they are still defending Israel so strongly? I think because this is such a personal and emotional journey, it is very hard for them to come to the realization that they were wrong and all their lives have been in a way, a myth.

IP: Yes and I think we should also point out that like in any colonialist situation where you have an anticolonialist struggle, there is a lot of violence in the air. When you are brought up in a certain way and the policies and actions of your own government push the other side to take some violent actions as well, then you think that objectively your point of view is correct because you see that there are suicide bombers, violence, missiles sent from Gaza. We also have to understand that this need to get out has been debated and examined within the context of permanent violence. It is very difficult for Israelis to separate between the violence and the experience and the reasons for that violence. One of the most difficult things is to explain to the Israelis what is the cause and what is the effect. What brings that violence about and not to regard this violence as just coming out of the blue and therefore they have no other choice than being where they are.

FB: That is the problem of knowledge and education. I think it also comes from the fact that mainstream media or the education system, in Israel even more, is not doing its job. When you hear people here saying: "What do you want Israel to do? Hamas has been sending one hundred and fifty rockets a day to Sderot, they have to react." I think in a time when history is very short term, we are not talking about six months, we are talking about last week, the circle of violence will never stop because the job is not done, the education part is not done.

IP: That's true and I think one of the major challenges is to find space for Israelis and Western people to be able to understand how it all began. Even the first Zionist settlers when they came and realized that what they thought was an empty land, or at least their own land, was full of Arab people, they regarded these people as aliens, as violent aliens who took over their land. It is this infrastructure they have built about the other side that feeds all the Israelis' perception and visions. It is a dehumanization of the Palestinians that begins in the late nineteenth century. How to explain to people that they are actually a product of this alienation? It is one of the biggest tasks for anyone who engages in alternative education or is trying to convey a different message to the Israeli Jews' society.

FB: I'd like you to talk about what historically was the first Palestinian Intifada of the late thirties, and the revolt against UK imperialism.

IP: I think it is important to go back to even earlier than 1936 in order to understand it. You have to go back to the late nineteenth century when Zionism appeared as a movement. It had two noble objectives: one was to find a safe place for Jews who felt insecure in a growing atmosphere of anti-Semitism, and the other was that some Jews wanted to redefine themselves in a national group, not just as a religion. The problem started when they chose Palestine as a territory in which to implement these two impulses. It was clear because the land was inhabited that you would have to do it by force and you had to contemplate the depopulation of the inhabitants of the indigenous people. It took time for the Palestinian community to realize that this was the plan. Even the Balfour declaration did not awaken the people when it was adopted in November 1917; it did not bring the Palestinians to revolt against the British policy or the Zionist strategy. By 1936, you could already see the beginning of the real result of this strategy: Palestinians were evicted from land purchased by the Zionist movement;

Palestinians lost their jobs because of Zionist strategy to take over the labor market. It was very clear that the European Jewish problem was going to be solved in Palestine. All these factors pushed Palestinians for the first time to say, "We are going to do something about it," and they tried to revolt. You needed the might of the British Empire to crush that revolt. It took them three years; they used the repertoire of actions against the Palestinians that were as bad as those that would be used later on by the Israelis to quell the Palestinian Intifadas of 1987 and 2000.

FB: This revolt of '36 was a very popular revolt; it was the "Falah," the peasants, that took arms. Also, in reading your books, I've realized that this revolt, being so violently squashed, did help the Haganah in '47/'48. The Palestinians were really weak at that time because all the leaders, all the potential fighting elements, had been killed or had to go into exile in 1936.

IP: Absolutely. The Palestinian political elite lived in cities of Palestine, but the main victims of Zionism up to the 1930s were in the countryside. That's why the revolt started there, but there were sections of the urban elite that joined them. Like you said, I pointed out in one of my books that the British killed or imprisoned most of those who belong to the Palestinian political elite and military or potentially military elite. They created a Palestinian society that was quite defenseless in 1947 when the first Zionist actions, with the knowledge that the British mandate came to an end, had commenced. I think it had an impact on the inability of the Palestinians to resist a year later in 1948 the ethnic cleansing of Palestine.

FB: Your work as a historian has helped to dismantle most of the myths about Israel. One of the myths is that Israel was created because the Bible gave it to the Jewish people. Could you to tell us a bit about Theodor Herzl, who is known as one of the founders of Zionism, was not religious at all, and did not speak even speak Yiddish?

IP: That's right. Zionism had one element that is usually forgotten by historians. This was a wish to secularize Jewish life. If you secularize the Jewish religion, you cannot later use the Bible as a justification for occupying Palestine. It was a bizarre mixture, which I like to call "a movement made by people who do not believe in God but God nonetheless promised them Palestine." I think this is something that is at the heart of the internal problems of Israeli Jewish society today. It is also important to understand that even before Herzl, there were people who thought about themselves as Zionists but were aware of the existence of Palestinians in Palestine. They were thinking of different kinds of connections to Palestine and solutions for the insecurity of Jews in Europe like Ahad Ha'Am (real name Asher Ginzburg), who said that maybe Palestine would just be a spiritual center and Jews, if they feel insecure in Europe, should settle elsewhere outside Europe or settle in more secure European societies. One important group of people that did not allow them to do this were Christian Zionists that already existed in those days who believed that the return of the Jews to Palestine was part of a divine scheme. They wanted the Jews to return to Palestine because they could precipitate the second coming of the Messiah; they were also anti-Semites. A "two for one" deal as they could also get rid of the Jews in Europe at the same time. I think it is an important period to go back to to understand how British imperialism, Christian Zionism, and of course

Jewish nationalism played together as a formidable force that left very few chances for the Palestinians when it all came together in the late nineteenth century.

FB: Like you said, you have to add anti–Semitism as well. When you hear Lord Balfour and the politicians at the time, they wanted the Jews to live in Palestine because they did not want the Jews in England or anywhere else in Europe.

History is crucial. We talked a few hours ago about knowledge and the way it is transmitted. Can you tell us about how history and knowledge, if it is properly taught, can enlighten people and can maybe better the struggle?

IP: I think we've already pointed it out. If you don't have a historical perspective, understanding, and if you don't know the facts, you accept the kind of negative depictions that the world and the Israelis have of Palestinians. I'll give you one example of what is so-called Palestinian terrorism that in the Israeli perspective and in some Western perspectives comes out of the blue: "We don't know why these people are violent, maybe it is because they are Muslims, maybe it is their political culture." It is only when you have a historical understanding that you can say, "Wait a minute, I understand where this violence comes from, I understand the source of the violence. Actually settling [in] my house by force is an act of violence. Maybe they were wrong, maybe they were right to try to resist by violence, but it begins by the very invasion of my space, the place where I live. This invasion is accompanied by a wish to get rid of me . . . what else can I do?" I think the historical dimension is important first for a better understanding of why the conflict continues. The second reason is that we will never succeed in changing political views about the Palestinian issue if we don't explain to people how knowledge was manipulated. It is very important because you need to understand how certain phrases are being used like *peace process*, how certain ideas are being broadcasted like *the only democracy in the Middle East*, like *Palestinian primitivism*, and so on. You need to understand how these languages are means of manipulating the knowledge that is there so as to form a certain point of view and prevent another point of view for coming into the space.

It's a twofold issue. You need to understand the history of the place but also the way the narratives have been constructed and how they are being manipulated and used. A crucial aspect is to understand how to challenge this. The main narrative that the Israelis are still successful in portraying is this idea of a land that even if it was not empty, was full of people who had no real connections to the place and are illegitimate. They lose legitimacy because they are not there, then they lose legitimacy because they are a bit of Bedouins and nomads so they don't really care, then they lose legitimacy by being violent or being Muslims after 9/11. There is all the time this laundry list of words and ideas that try to convince you that whatever the Israelis are doing, if you are unhappy with this, it doesn't matter because there is no one on the other side that has anything legitimate to offer—it all depends on the Israelis' kindness. If you check very carefully the language of peace since Oslo, even before—but it has been more accentuated since Oslo—it is all about Israeli concessions. The language is *concession*, Israelis will make concessions to Palestinians and then, there is a chance for peace. If this is the departure point, there will never be any reconciliation. "I invaded your house, but I am generous enough to let you come back and take the sofa with you to the new place." That is hardly a dialogue that wants to settle a conflict; it is almost more humiliating than the act of invasion itself.

FB: Historians are subjective, right? For example, how can you and Benny Morris agree on the facts of '47/'48 but come to very different conclusions? How do you deal with that?

IP: First of all, I think there is a factual infrastructure. We all have to know it and in this respect it is good that Benny Morris at least headed the charge to voice this idea that you should stop the nonsense of saying that Palestinians left voluntarily in 1948. This was a factual debate: did they leave voluntarily or were they expelled? What you feel from this debate when it continues is that this is not the most important issue because before historians appeared in Israel, we knew that Palestinians were being expelled, we just did not believe the Palestinians. There were five million Palestinian refugees who kept telling us, "We were expelled," and we said, "No, you are Palestinians. When you say it, we don't believe you." It is only when the Israeli historians came to say, "You know what? They are right," they had documents that confirmed what the Palestinians were saying that suddenly they were telling the truth. This was only a first step, the more important thing was not what happened, but what to learn from what happened. What are our conclusions? This is a moral and ideological debate. The artificial attempt to say that historians can only deal with what happened and not say anything about what the implications are constitute false approaches that can be seen in Morris's own work. He writes in his first book that he is a bit sorry for what has been done in 1948, and in his last book, he is sorry that the Israelis did not complete the ethnic cleansing. He has not changed one fact in both books. They are the same facts, but the books are being written very differently: one book doesn't like the idea of an ethnic cleansing, the other book endorses it—not only justifies it in the past, but endorses it as a plan for the future.

Florent Barat: It's time for a musical break. Ilan, you've chosen two tracks that you wanted to listen to. Could you introduce the first one and maybe tell us the reasons why you've chosen this one?

IP: The first track is a song by Cat Stevens; it is called "Peace Train." I've always loved Cat Stevens. I am a product of the seventies and he is one of my musical heroes. I also like his very bold move by converting to Islam and not being terrified by everything that was said about him. I think there is some honesty in this guy. This song, for me, was encapsulating although I'm not sure he meant the same things that I mean, but that doesn't matter! It encapsulates what I was always longing for, to have this peace train coming to Israel and Palestine. You have to understand who is the driver and who are the passengers. I wrote in one of my articles (I can't remember which one) that there is a difference between a peace train that takes us all to a better destination, which is the peace process that we don't have, and the peace train that runs over everyone on the way to the so-called peace, which I think is our present peace process so it is a very powerful metaphor for me.

FB: You moved to Exeter in the UK in 2007 but still go back to Israel very often. How has the situation evolved in Israel in the last few years?

IP: The task of changing Jewish society from within is formidable. This society seems to be more and more entrenched on its positions. The more I think about it the more desperate I am about succeeding in changing it from within. On the other side there is a growing number of young people who seem to grasp reality in a different way. There are very few, but I do not remember having such a young generation before in Israel. So although the short-term future does not harbor any chance for a change from within, there are signs that with pressure from outside, there is a group of people there with whom one will be able in the future potentially to create a different society. If you compare Israel today with the Israel I left, or the Israel I grew up in, the trend is to become more chauvinistic, ethnocentric, intransigent, which makes us all feel that peace and reconciliation are very far away if we only rely on our hope that Jewish society will change from within.

FB: Should we therefore put all our energy on applying pressure from the outside or should we still try to talk to Israelis to help them change their views?

IP: The reason why we are all debating this is because on the ground the machine of destruction does not stop for one day. We therefore don't have the luxury to wait any longer. Time is not on our side. We know that while we wait, many terrible things are happening. We also now there is a correlation between those terrible things happening and the realization of the Israelis that there is a price tag attached to what they are doing. If they pay no price for what they are doing, they will even accelerate the strategy of ethnic cleansing. It's therefore a mixture. We urgently need to find a system by which you stop what is being done now, on the ground, and to also prevent what is about to happen. You need a powerful model of pressure from the outside. As far as people from the outside are concerned, international civil society, I think the BDS movement is as good as it gets. Still, it can't be the only model or factor. There are two additional factors to make it a successful process. One is on the Palestinian side. The question of representation needs to be sorted. You need a good solution. Secondly, you need to have a kind of educational system, inside, that takes the time to educate the Israeli Jews about a different reality and the benefit it will bring to them. If those factors all work well together, and we have a more holistic approach to the question of reconciliation, things could change.

Florent Barat: As a teacher, wouldn't you be more useful teaching in Israel than abroad? Could you be the teacher you are in the UK in Israel?

IP: I don't think I want to be a teacher in a university anyway. Universities are not the best place to teach people about the realities of life or can change their point of view. Universities are sites for careers now, not for knowledge and education. I am teaching in Israel as well, in my own way, through my articles, through the tiny amount of public speaking I am allowed to do. I would like to continue this. I feel like what I am doing in Britain is working on the pressure from the outside less than education. You cannot sustain a BDS campaign without explaining to people why it is necessary, to give them the tools and the background they need to understand it. To legitimize it. We do not cease to be educators as well as activists all the time. It's important to try to combine and find the time for the actions that you take and the educational process. We can't be too impatient if people do not get it straight away. We have to be patient and explain our positions again and again until people understand them.

FB: I am very interested in the question of solidarity. About its real meaning. What does solidarity mean for non-Palestinians? Whom do we stand in solidarity with? What about if whoever represents the Palestinians decides that they want a state on 11 percent of historical Palestine and that they want a neoliberal, capitalist state. How am I supposed to stand in solidarity with that?

IP: First of all, the solidarity is with victims of a certain policy and ideology even if these victims are not represented. You are in solidarity with their suffering and you support their attempt to get out of this suffering. Now, you raise an interesting question. I think that part of solidarity is like a good friendship. As a good friend, you can tell your friend that you understand what he is doing, but that you think he is wrong. Those of us in solidarity with the Palestinian people, we find ourselves, when it comes to our debates with good friends that still support the peace process, the two-state solution, disagreeing with them. Part of our role is to tell them that we think they are wrong. The assumption in your question is not realistic. Not one Palestinian will ever agree with that. Still, if that happens, yes, maybe we will have to rethink the whole idea of solidarity. Those debates are organic and stem from the situation; we are not inventing them. If you have a position between one state or two states or what kind of means the Palestinians should adopt, you connect to issues the Palestinians have themselves, you're therefore not an outsider. You will be betraying your solidarity if you stopped having a position on the current and important debates. I know that sometimes there is a nationalistic position saying that because you're not Palestinian, you cannot comment and are not entitled to have an opinion. For me, movements are made of people and people are different from one another. Not everybody is going to play according to the same rules. I think that solidarity is also agreeing on what is right and what is wrong to do. What are the boundaries of the involvement of people from the outside? There is no dogmatic answer to this. Usually when someone says something like "You cannot advocate one state if you're not Palestinian or Israeli," it's usually to stifle a debate. We should not waste too much time on this question. By now I think that everyone involved knows what solidarity means and what it entitles you to do.

FB: Let's talk about the "solution." Is there really a debate right now about this? The two-state solution as far as the institutions are concerned, the governments, still seems to be the only solution on the table. When you mention one state, people either call you a utopian or say that you are against Jewish self-determination. Even the so-called Palestinian political leaders, despite what's happening on the ground, still support a two-state solution. The more rational and humane solution, which would be one state, is still not debated and thought about enough in terms of the practicalities of it, the how to get there.

IP: I think two things are taking place. One is the issue of Palestinian representativity. The people who claim to represent the Palestinians from the West Bank became the representatives of the whole Palestinian people. As far as the West Bank is concerned, you see why a two-state solution is attractive. It could mean the end of military control in their lives. One can understand this. But this disregards the other Palestinians. The refugees, the ones from Gaza and the ones that live inside Israel. That's one of the difficulties. You have certain groups of Palestinians that, in my opinion, wrongly believe that this is the quickest way to end the occupation.

I don't think it is. You're right when you are saying the Oslo agreement ensured the continuation of the occupation, not the end of it. The second reason is that the two-state solution has a logical ring to it. It's a very Western idea. A colonialist invention that was applied in India and Africa, this idea of partition, while the non-Western world is a far more holistic world. [The idea of partition] became a kind of religion to the extent that you do not question it anymore. You work out how best to get there. To my mind it makes very intelligent people take this as a religion of logic. If you question the rationality of it, you are criticized. This is while a lot of people in the West stick to it. Nothing on the ground would ever change their mind. Of course you're right. Five minutes on the ground shows you that one state is already there. It's a non-democratic regime, an apartheid regime. So you just need to think about how to change this regime. You do not need to think about a two-state solution. You need to think about how to change the relations between the communities, how to affect the power structure in place.

FB: Right. So, as you're saying, why are very intelligent people, very rational ones, still saying that the two-state solution is the compulsory step, the first unavoidable one, toward something better? I went to lectures about this, but I still don't get it. How would this work in practice?

IP: Again, it goes back to a rationalist Western way to look at reality. It says that I can only advocate for what I can get, not what I want. At this moment in time it seems that you have such a wide coalition for a two-state solution, so you go for it. You do not evaluate its morality, its ethical dimension, even if it's likely to change the reality later on. This whole idea that this is a very reasonable approach is of course reasonable to a point. But it's totally insane because it has nothing to do with the conflict. It has to do with the way Israel wants the world to accept this idea, constructed in 1967, that it needs most of the territory that it occupied then, but that it is willing to allow some autonomy to the Palestinians in that territory. That's the debate in Israel. It's never about the principles. The thing that Israel has always needed is international support. They need their policies rubber-stamped by the international community. They also need a Palestinian representative. In 1993 the PLO surprised them when it agreed to have a small autonomous area on a small part of the West Bank and leave all the rest to Israel. That's the two-state solution that everybody wants to convince us is the only way forward. The problem is that not one Palestinian can live with this, hence the continuation of the conflict.

FB: Edward Said died ten years ago. He was one of the last Palestinians, with Mahmoud Darwish, that the majority of the Palestinians looked up to. I know you knew him well. Can you end by giving us a few words on Edward Said and the role he played during his life?

IP: We miss him very much. I don't think only Palestinians looked up to him for inspiration. He was one of the greatest intellectuals of the second half of the last century. We all looked at him for inspiration. On questions of knowledge, morality, inspiration, activism, not only on Palestine. We are missing his holistic approach. His ability to see things from above in a more wholesome way. When you lose someone like that, you have people that are taking the fragmentation that Israel imposes on the Palestinians and act as if this is a reality itself. What we need is to overcome the intellectual, physical, and cultural fragmentation that Israel imposes on us, Palestinians and Jews, and to strive to come back to something far more organic and integrated so that the third generation of Jewish settlers and indigenous native people of Palestine could have a future together.

Florent Barat: Final question now: Ilan, are you working on a book right now?

IP: I've got several in fact. One of them is coming out next winter. It's called *The Idea of Israel* (Verso). It's a history of the production of knowledge in Israel. In 2015 my book on Israel's history of the occupation of the West Bank, called *Mega Prison of Palestine*, will come out.

CHAPTER SIX

Inside the United States

FB: What is the definition of negotiations in Israel-US language and why is the Palestinian Authority playing along?

NC: From the US point of view, negotiations are, in effect, a way for Israel to continue its policies of systematically taking over whatever it wants in the West Bank, maintaining the brutal siege on Gaza, separating Gaza from the West Bank and, of course, occupying the Syrian Golan Heights, all with full US support. And the framework of negotiations, as in the past twenty years of the Oslo experience, has simply provided a cover for this.

FB: Why is the PA playing along with this and going to negotiations time after time?

NC: It's probably partly out of desperation. You can ask whether it's the right choice or not, but they don't have many alternatives.

This conversation between Noam Chomsky and Frank Barat was recorded September 6, 2013, and has been condensed and edited. Originally published September 7, 2013, at *Ceasefire* magazine.

FB: So in your opinion it's pretty much to survive that they indeed accept the framework?

NC: If they were to refuse to join the US-run negotiations, their basis for support would collapse. They survive on donations essentially. Israel has made sure that it's not a productive economy. They're a kind of what would be called in Yiddish a *schnorrer* society: you just borrow and live on what you can get.

Whether they have an alternative to that is not so clear, but if they were to refuse the US demand for negotiations on completely unacceptable terms, their basis for support would erode. And they *do* have support—external support—enough so that the Palestinian elite can live a fairly decent, often lavish, lifestyle, while the society around them collapses.

FB: So would the crumbling and disappearance of the PA be a bad thing after all?

NC: It depends on what would replace it. If, say, Marwan Barghouti were permitted to join the society the way, say, Nelson Mandela was finally, that could have a revitalizing effect in organizing a Palestinian society that might press for more substantial demands. But remember: they don't have a lot of choices.

In fact, go back to the beginning of the Oslo agreements, now twenty years old. There *were* negotiations under way, the Madrid negotiations, at which the Palestinian delegation was led by Haider Abdel-Shafi, a highly respected, left-nationalist figure in Palestine. He was refusing to agree to the US-Israel terms, which required crucially that settlement expansion be allowed to continue. He refused, and therefore the negotiations stalled and got nowhere.

Meanwhile Arafat and the external Palestinians went on the side track through Oslo, gained control, and Haider Abdel-Shafi was so opposed to this he didn't even show up to the dramatic and meaningless ceremony where Clinton beamed while Arafat and Rabin shook hands. He didn't show up because he realized it was a total sellout. But he was principled and therefore could get nowhere, and *we'll* get nowhere unless there's substantial support from the European Union, the Gulf States, and ultimately, from the United States.

FB: In your opinion what is really at stake in what's unraveling in Syria at the moment, and what does it mean for the broader region?

NC: Well, Syria is descending into suicide. It's a horror story and getting worse and worse. There's no bright spot on the horizon. What will probably happen, if this continues, is that Syria will be partitioned into probably three regions: a Kurdish region—which is already forming—that could pull out and join in some fashion the semi-autonomous Iraqi Kurdistan, maybe with some kind of deal with Turkey.

The rest of the country will be divided between a region dominated by the Assad regime—a brutal, horrifying regime—and another section dominated by the various militias, which range from the extremely malicious and violent to the secular and democratic. Meanwhile, Israel is looking on and enjoying the spectacle.

For the United States, that's fine, they don't want an outcome either. If the US and Israel wanted to assist the rebels—which they do not—they can do it, even without military intervention. For example, if Israel were to mobilize forces on the Golan Heights—of course, it's the *Syrian* Golan Heights, but by now the world more or less tolerates or accepts Israel's illegal occupation—if they would just do that, it would compel Assad to move forces to the south, which would relieve pressure against the rebels. But there's no hint even of that. They're also not giving humanitarian aid to the huge number of suffering refugees, not doing all kinds of simple things that they could do.

All of which suggests that both Israel and the United States prefer exactly what is happening today. Meanwhile, Israel can celebrate its status as what they call a "villa in the jungle." There was an interesting article by the editor of *Haaretz*, Aluf Benn, who wrote about how Israelis are going to the beach and enjoying themselves, and congratulating themselves on being a "villa in the jungle" while the wild beasts out there tear each other to shreds. And, of course, Israel in this picture is doing nothing except defending itself. They like that picture and the US doesn't seem too dissatisfied with it either. The rest is shadowboxing.

FB: What about talk of a US strike then; do you think it's going to happen?
NC: A bombing?

FB: Yes.
NC: Well, it's kind of an interesting debate in the United States. The ultra-Right, the right-wing extremists, who are kind of off the international spectrum, they're opposing it, though not for reasons I like. They're opposing it because "Why should we dedicate ourselves to solving other people's problems and waste our own resources?" They're literally asking, "Who's going to defend us when we're attacked, because we're devoting ourselves to helping people overseas?" That's the ultra-Right. If you look at the

"moderate" Right, people like, say, David Brooks of the *New York Times*, considered an intellectual commentator on the right. His view is that the US effort to withdraw its forces from the region is not having a "moderating effect." According to Brooks, when US forces are in the region, that has a moderating effect; it improves the situation, as you can see in Iraq, for example. But if we're withdrawing our forces, then we're no longer able to moderate the situation and make it better.

That's the standard view from the intellectual right over to the mainstream, the liberal Democrats, and so on. So there's a lot of talk about "Should we exercise our 'responsibility to protect'?" Well, just take a look at the US record on "responsibility to protect" [R2P]. The fact that these words can even be spoken reveals something quite extraordinary about the US—and, in fact, Western—moral and intellectual culture.

This is quite apart from the fact that it's a gross violation of international law. Obama's latest line is that *he* didn't establish a "red line," but the world did through its conventions on chemical warfare. Well, actually, the world *does* have a treaty, which Israel didn't sign and which the US has totally neglected, for example when it supported Saddam Hussein's really horrifying use of chemical weapons. Today, this is used to denounce Saddam Hussein, overlooking the fact that it was not only tolerated but basically supported by the Reagan administration. And, of course, the convention has no enforcement mechanisms.

There's also no such thing as "responsibility to protect," that's a fraud perpetrated in Western intellectual culture. There *is* a *notion*, in fact two notions: there's one passed by the UN General Assembly, which does talk about a "responsibility to protect," but it offers no authorization for any kind of intervention except under conditions of the United Nations charter. There is another version, which is adopted only by the West, the US, and its allies, which is unilateral and says R2P permits "military intervention by regional organizations in the region of their authority without Security Council authorization."

Well, translating that into English, this means that it provides authorization for the US and NATO to use violence wherever they choose without Security Council authorization. That's what's called "responsibility to protect" in Western discourse. If it weren't so tragic, it would be farcical.

PART TWO

Reflections

CHAPTER SEVEN

Gaza's Torment, Israel's Crimes, Our Responsibilities

Noam Chomsky

At 3 a.m. Gaza time, July 9, 2014, in the midst of Israel's latest exercise in savagery, I received a phone call from a young Palestinian journalist in Gaza. In the background, I could hear his infant child wailing, amid the sounds of explosions and jet planes, targeting any civilian who moves, and homes as well. He just saw a friend of his in a car clearly marked "press" get blown away. And he heard shrieks next door after an explosion but couldn't go outside or he'd be a likely target. This is a quiet neighborhood, no military targets—except Palestinians who are fair game for Israel's high-tech US-supplied military machine. He said that 70 percent of the ambulances have been destroyed, and that by then more than seventy had been killed, and of the three hundred or so wounded, about two-thirds were women and children. Few

Originally published in *Z* magazine, July 12, 2014.

Hamas activists or rocket launching sites have been hit—just the usual victims.

It is important to understand what life is like in Gaza when Israel's behavior is "restrained," in between the regular manufactured crises like this one. A good sense is given in a report to the United Nations Relief and Works Agency (UNRWA) by Mads Gilbert, the courageous and expert Norwegian physician who has worked extensively in Gaza, including throughout the vicious and murderous Cast Lead operation. In every respect, the situation is disastrous. Just keeping to children, Gilbert reports: "Palestinian children in Gaza are suffering immensely. A large proportion are affected by the man-made malnourishment regime caused by the Israeli imposed blockage. Prevalence of anaemia in children under 2 years in Gaza is at 72.8 percent, while prevalence of wasting, stunting, underweight have been documented at 34.3 percent, 31.4 percent, 31.45 percent respectively." And it gets worse as the report proceeds.

When Israel is on "good behavior," more than two Palestinian children are killed every week, a pattern that goes back over fourteen years. The underlying cause is the criminal occupation and the programs to reduce Palestinian life to bare survival in Gaza, while Palestinians are restricted to unviable cantons in the West Bank and Israel takes over what it wants, all in gross violation of international law and explicit Security Council resolutions, not to speak of minimal decency. And it will continue as long as it is supported by Washington and tolerated by Europe—to our everlasting shame.

CHAPTER EIGHT

A Brief History of Israel's Incremental Genocide

Ilan Pappé

In a September 2006 article for the *Electronic Intifada*, I defined the Israeli policy toward the Gaza Strip as an incremental genocide.

Israel's present assault on Gaza alas indicates that this policy continues unabated. The term is important since it appropriately locates Israel's barbaric action—then and now—within a wider historical context.

People in Gaza and elsewhere in Palestine feel disappointed at the lack of any significant international reaction to the carnage and destruction the Israeli assault has so far left behind in the Strip. The inability, or unwillingness, to act seems to be first and foremost an acceptance of the Israeli narrative and argumentation for the crisis in Gaza. Israel has developed a very clear narrative

---

Adapted from "Israel's Incremental Genocide in the Gaza Ghetto," *Electronic Intifada,* July 13, 2014, and "The Historical Perspective of the 2014 Gaza Massacre," *Information Clearing House,* August 23, 2014.

about the present carnage in Gaza: it is a tragedy caused by an unprovoked Hamas missile attack on the Jewish state, to which Israel had to react in self-defense.

While mainstream Western media, academia, and politicians may have reservations about the proportionality of the force used by Israel, they accept the gist of this argument. This Israeli narrative is totally rejected in the world of cyber-activism and alternative media. There it seems the condemnation of the Israeli action as a war crime is widespread and consensual.

The main difference between the two analyses (from above and from below) is the willingness of activists to study deeper and in a more profound way the ideological and historical context of the present Israeli action in Gaza. A historical evaluation and contextualization of the present Israeli assault on Gaza and that of the previous three since 2006 expose clearly the Israeli genocidal policy there. An incremental policy of massive killing that is less a product of a callous intention and more the inevitable outcome of Israel's overall strategy toward Palestine in general and the areas it occupied in 1967 in particular.

This context should be insisted upon, since the Israeli propaganda machine attempts again and again to narrate its policies as out of context and turns the pretext it found for every previous wave of destruction into the main justification for another spree of indiscriminate slaughter in the killing fields of Palestine.

The Zionist strategy of branding its brutal policies as an ad hoc response to this or that Palestinian action is as old as the Zionist presence in Palestine itself. It was used repeatedly as a justification for implementing the Zionist vision of a future Palestine that has in it very few, if any, native Palestinians.

The means for achieving this goal has changed over the years, but the formula has remained the same: whatever the Zionist vision of a Jewish state might be, it can only materialize without any significant number of Palestinians in it. And nowadays the vision is of an Israel stretching over almost the whole of historic Palestine where millions of Palestinians still live.

The present genocidal wave has, like all the previous ones, also a more immediate background. It has been born out of an attempt to foil the Palestinian decision to form a unity government that even the United States could not object to.

The collapse of US secretary of state John Kerry's desperate "peace" initiative legitimized the Palestinian appeal to international organizations to stop the occupation. At the same time, Palestinians gained wide international blessing for the cautious attempt represented by the unity government to strategize once again a coordinated policy among the various Palestinian groups and agendas.

Ever since June 1967, Israel has searched for a way to keep the territories it occupied that year without incorporating their indigenous Palestinian population into its rights-bearing citizenry. All the while it participated in a "peace process" charade to cover up or buy time for its unilateral colonization policies on the ground.

In the last few decades, Israel differentiated between areas it wished to control directly and those it would manage indirectly, with the aim in the long run of downsizing the Palestinian population to a minimum through, among other means, ethnic cleansing and economic and geographic strangulation. Thus the West Bank was in effect divided into "Jewish" and "Palestinian" zones—a reality most Israelis can live with provided the Palestinian bantustans' inhabitants are content with their incarceration within these mega-prisons. The geopolitical location of the West Bank creates the impression in Israel, at least, that it is possible to achieve this without anticipating a third uprising or too much international condemnation.

The Gaza Strip, due to its unique geopolitical location, did not lend itself that easily to such a strategy. Ever since 1994, and even more so when Ariel Sharon came to power as prime minister in the early 2000s, the strategy there has been to ghettoize Gaza and somehow hope that the people there—1.8 million as of today— would be dropped into eternal oblivion.

But the ghetto proved to be rebellious and unwilling to live under conditions of strangulation, isolation, starvation, and economic collapse. There was no way it would be annexed to Egypt, either in 1948 or in 2014. In 1948, Israel pushed into the Gaza area (before it became a strip) hundreds of thousands of refugees it expelled from the northern Naqab and southern coast who, so Israel hoped, would move even farther away from Palestine.

For a while after 1967, Israel wanted to keep the West Bank as a township which provided unskilled labor but without any human and civil rights. When the occupied people resisted the continued oppression in two intifadas, the West Bank was bisected into small bantustans encircled by Jewish colonies, but it did not work in the too-small and too-dense Gaza Strip. The Israelis were unable to "West Bank" the Strip, so to speak. So they cordoned it as a ghetto and when it resisted, the army was allowed to use its most formidable and lethal weapons to crush it. The inevitable result of an accumulative reaction of this kind was genocidal.

On May 15, Israeli forces killed two Palestinian youths in the West Bank town of Beitunia, their cold-blooded slayings by a sniper's bullet captured on video. Their names—Nadim Nuwara and Muhammad Abu al-Thahir—were added to a long list of such killings in recent months and years.

The killing of three Israeli teenagers, two of them minors, abducted in the occupied West Bank in June, was perhaps in reprisal for killings of Palestinian children. But for all the depredations of the oppressive occupation, it provided the pretext first and foremost for destroying the delicate unity in the West Bank, a unity that followed a decision by the Palestinian Authority to forsake the "peace process" and appeal to international organizations to judge Israel according to a human and civil rights' yardstick. Both developments were viewed as alarming in Israel.

The abductions also created the pretext for the implementation of the old dream of wiping out Hamas from Gaza so that the ghetto could be quiet again.

Since 1994, even before the rise of Hamas to power in the Gaza Strip, the very particular geopolitical location of the Strip has made it clear that any collective punitive action, such as the one inflicted now, could only be an operation of massive killings and destruction—in other words, of a continued genocide.

This recognition never inhibited the generals who give the orders to bomb the people from the air, the sea, and the ground. Downsizing the number of Palestinians all over historic Palestine is still the Zionist vision. In Gaza, its implementation takes its most inhuman form.

The particular timing of this genocidal wave is determined, as in the past, by additional considerations. The domestic social unrest of 2011 is still simmering and for a while there was a public demand to cut military expenditures and move money from the inflated "defense" budget to social services. The army branded this possibility as suicidal. There is nothing like a military operation to stifle any voices calling on the government to cut its military expenses.

Typical hallmarks of the previous stages in this incremental genocide reappear in this wave as well. One can witness again consensual Israeli Jewish support for the massacre of civilians in the Gaza Strip without one significant voice of dissent. In Tel Aviv, the few who dared to demonstrate against it were beaten by Jewish hooligans, while the police stood by and watched.

Academia, as always, becomes part of the machinery. The prestigious private university, the Interdisciplinary Center Herzliya, has established a "civilian headquarters" where students volunteer to serve as mouthpieces in the propaganda campaign abroad. Various universities have offered the state their student bodies to help and battle for the Israeli narrative in cyberspace and the alternative media.

The Israeli media, as well, has toed loyally the government's line, showing no pictures of the human catastrophe Israel has wreaked and informing its public that this time, "The world understands us and is behind us." That statement is valid to a point as the political elites in the West continue to provide the old immunity to the Jewish state. The recent appeal by Western governments to the prosecutor in the International Court of Justice in The Hague not to look into Israel's crimes in Gaza is a case in point. Wide sections of the Western media have followed suit and have justified by and large Israel's actions—including the

French media, especially France 24, and the BBC, which continue to shamefully parrot Israeli propaganda. This is not surprising, since pro-Israel lobby groups continue to work tirelessly to press Israel's case in France and the rest of Europe as they do in the United States.

This distorted coverage is also fed by a sense among Western journalists that what happens in Gaza pales in comparison to the atrocities in Iraq and Syria. Comparisons like this are usually provided without a wider historical perspective. A longer view on the history of the Palestinians would be a much more appropriate way to evaluate their suffering vis-à-vis the carnage elsewhere.

But not only a historical view is needed for a better understanding of the massacre in Gaza; a dialectical approach that identifies the connection between Israel's immunity and the horrific developments elsewhere is required as well. The dehumanization in Iraq and Syria is widespread and terrifying, as it is in Gaza. But there is one crucial difference between these cases and the Israeli brutality: the former are condemned as barbarous and inhuman worldwide, while those committed by Israel are still publicly licensed and approved by the president of the United States, the leaders of the European Union, and Israel's other friends in the world.

Whether it is burning alive a Palestinian youth from Jerusalem, fatally shooting two others just for the fun of it in Beitunia, or slaying whole families in Gaza, these are all acts that can only be perpetrated if the victim is dehumanized. The only chance for a successful struggle against Zionism in Palestine is the one based on a human and civil rights agenda that does not differentiate between one violation and the other and yet identifies clearly the victim and the victimizers.

Those who commit atrocities in the Arab world against oppressed minorities and helpless communities, as well as the Israelis who commit these crimes against the Palestinian people, should all be judged by the same moral and ethical standards. They are all war criminals, though in the case of Palestine they have been at work longer than anyone else. It does not really matter what the religious identity is of the people who commit the atrocities or in the name of which religion they purport to speak. Whether they call themselves jihadists, Judaists, or Zionists, they should be treated in the same way.

A world that would stop employing double standards in its dealings with Israel is a world that could be far more effective in its response to war crimes elsewhere in the world.

The cessation of the incremental genocide in Gaza and the restitution of the basic human and civil rights of Palestinians wherever they are, including the right of return, is the only way to open a new vista for a productive international intervention in the Middle East as a whole.

CHAPTER NINE

Nightmare in Gaza

Noam Chomsky

Amid all the horrors unfolding in the latest Israeli offensive in Gaza, Israel's goal is simple: "quiet for quiet," a return to the norm.

For the West Bank, the norm is that Israel continues its illegal construction of settlements and infrastructure so that it can integrate into Israel whatever might be of value, meanwhile consigning Palestinians to unviable cantons and subjecting them to repression and violence.

For Gaza, the norm is a miserable existence under a cruel and destructive siege that Israel administers to permit bare survival but nothing more.

For the past fourteen years, the norm is that Israel kills more than two Palestinian children a week.

The latest Israeli rampage was set off by the brutal murder of three Israeli boys from a settler community in the occupied West

---

Adapted from "Nightmare in Gaza," *AlterNet*, August 1, 2014, and "Outrage," *Information Clearing House*, August 3, 2014.

Bank. A month before, two Palestinian boys were shot dead in the West Bank city of Ramallah. That elicited little attention, which is understandable, since it is routine.

"The institutionalized disregard for Palestinian life in the West helps explain not only why Palestinians resort to violence," Middle East analyst Mouin Rabbani reports, "but also Israel's latest assault on the Gaza Strip."

"Quiet for quiet" also enables Israel to carry forward its program of separating Gaza from the West Bank. That program has been pursued vigorously, always with US support, ever since the US and Israel accepted the Oslo Accords, which declare the two regions to be an inseparable territorial unity. A look at the map explains the rationale. Gaza provides Palestine's only access to the outside world, so once the two are separated, any autonomy that Israel might grant to Palestinians in the West Bank would leave them effectively imprisoned between hostile states, Israel and Jordan. The imprisonment will become even more severe as Israel continues its program of expelling Palestinians from the Jordan Valley and constructing Israeli settlements there.

The norm in Gaza was described in detail by the heroic Norwegian trauma surgeon Mads Gilbert, who has worked in Gaza's main hospital through Israel's most grotesque crimes and returned again for the current onslaught. In June 2014 he submitted a report on the Gaza health sector to the UNRWA, the UN agency that tries desperately, on a shoestring, to care for refugees.

"At least 57 percent of Gaza households are food insecure and about 80 percent are now aid recipients," Gilbert reports. "Food insecurity and rising poverty also mean that most residents cannot meet their daily caloric requirements, while over 90 percent of the water in Gaza has been deemed unfit for human consumption," a situation that is becoming even worse as Israel again attacks water and sewage systems, leaving 1.2 million people with even more severe disruption of the barest necessity of life.

In an interview, human rights lawyer Raji Sourani, who has remained in Gaza through years of Israeli brutality and terror, said, "The most common sentence I heard when people began to talk about cease-fire: Everybody says it's better for all of us to die and not go back to the situation we used to have before this war. We don't want that again. We have no dignity, no pride; we are just soft targets, and we are very cheap. Either this situation really improves or it is better to just die. I am talking about intellectuals, academics, ordinary people: Everybody is saying that."

Similar sentiments have been widely heard: it is better to die with dignity than to be slowly strangled by the torturer.

For Gaza, the plans for the norm were explained forthrightly by Dov Weissglass, the confidant of Ariel Sharon who negotiated the withdrawal of Israeli settlers from Gaza in 2005. Hailed as a grand gesture in Israel and among acolytes and the deluded elsewhere, the withdrawal was in reality a carefully staged "national trauma," properly ridiculed by informed Israeli commentators, among them Israel's leading sociologist, the late Baruch Kimmerling.

What actually happened is that Israeli hawks, led by Sharon, realized that it made good sense to transfer the illegal settlers from their subsidized communities in devastated Gaza to subsidized settlements in the other occupied territories, which Israel intends to keep. But instead of simply transferring them, as would have been simple enough, it was considered more effective to present the world with images of little children pleading with soldiers not to destroy their homes, amid cries of "Never Again," with the implication obvious. What made the farce even more transparent was that it was a replica of the staged trauma when Israel had to evacuate the Egyptian Sinai in 1982. But it played very well for the intended audience abroad.

In Weissglass's own description of the transfer of settlers from Gaza to other occupied territories, "What I effectively agreed to with the Americans was that [the major settlement blocs in the West Bank] would not be dealt with at all, and the rest will not be dealt with until the Palestinians turn into Finns"—but a special kind of Finns, who would accept rule by a foreign power. "The significance is the freezing of the political process," Weissglass continued. "And when you freeze that process you prevent the establishment of a Palestinian state and you prevent a discussion about the refugees, the borders, and Jerusalem. Effectively, this whole package that is called the Palestinian state, with all that it entails, has been removed from our agenda indefinitely. And all this with [George W. Bush's] authority and permission and the ratification of both houses of Congress."

Weisglass added that Gazans would remain "on a diet, but not to make them die of hunger"—which would not help Israel's fading reputation. With their vaunted technical efficiency, Israeli experts determined exactly how many calories a day Gazans needed for bare survival, while also depriving them of medicines, construction materials, or other means of decent life. Israeli military forces confined them by land, sea, and air to what British prime minister David Cameron accurately described as a prison camp. The Israeli withdrawal left Israel in total control of Gaza, hence the occupying power under international law.

The official story is that after Israel graciously handed Gaza over to the Palestinians, in the hope that they would construct a flourishing state, they revealed their true nature by subjecting Israel to unremitting rocket attack and forcing the captive population to become martyrs, leaving Israel in a bad light for failing to anticipate this scenario. Reality is rather different.

In January 2006, Palestinians committed a major crime: they voted the wrong way in a carefully monitored free election, handing control of Parliament to Hamas. The media constantly intone that Hamas is dedicated to the destruction of Israel. In reality, Hamas leaders have repeatedly made it clear that Hamas would accept a two-state settlement in accord with the international consensus that has been blocked by the United States and Israel for forty years. In contrast, Israel is dedicated to the destruction of Palestine, apart from some occasional meaningless words, and is implementing that commitment.

True, Israel accepted the road map for reaching a two-state settlement initiated by President George W. Bush and adopted by the Quartet that is to supervise it: the United States, the European Union, the United Nations, and Russia. But as he accepted the road map, Prime Minister Sharon at once added fourteen reservations that effectively nullify it. The facts were known to activists, but revealed to the general public for the first time in Jimmy Carter's book *Palestine: Peace Not Apartheid*. They remain under wraps in media reporting and commentary.

The (unrevised) 1999 platform of Israel's governing party, Benjamin Netanyahu's Likud, "flatly rejects the establishment of a Palestinian Arab state west of the Jordan river." And for those who like to obsess about meaningless charters, the core component of

Likud, Menachem Begin's Herut, has yet to abandon its founding doctrine that the territory on both sides of the Jordan is part of the Land of Israel.

The crime of the Palestinians in January 2006 was punished at once. The United States and Israel, with Europe shamefully trailing behind, imposed harsh sanctions on the errant population and Israel stepped up its violence. The United States and Israel quickly initiated plans for a military coup to overthrow the elected government. When Hamas had the effrontery to foil the plans, the Israeli assaults and the siege became far more severe.

There should be no need to review again the dismal record since. The relentless siege and savage attacks are punctuated by episodes of "mowing the lawn," to borrow Israel's cheery expression for its periodic exercises in shooting fish in a pond as part of what it calls a "war of defense."

Once the lawn is mowed and the desperate population seeks to rebuild somehow from the devastation and the murders, there is a ceasefire agreement. The most recent ceasefire was established after Israel's October 2012 assault, called Operation Pillar of Defense.

Though Israel maintained its siege, Hamas observed the ceasefire, as Israel concedes. Matters changed in April of this year when Fatah and Hamas forged a unity agreement that established a new government of technocrats unaffiliated with either party.

Israel was naturally furious, all the more so when even the Obama administration joined the West in signaling approval. The unity agreement not only undercuts Israel's claim that it cannot negotiate with a divided Palestine but also threatens the long-term goal of dividing Gaza from the West Bank and pursuing its destructive policies in both regions.

Something had to be done, and an occasion arose on June 12, when the three Israeli boys were murdered in the West Bank. Early on, the Netanyahu government knew that they were dead, but pretended otherwise, which provided the opportunity to launch a rampage in the West Bank, targeting Hamas.

Prime Minister Netanyahu claimed to have certain knowledge that Hamas was responsible. That too was a lie.

One of Israel's leading authorities on Hamas, Shlomi Eldar, reported almost at once that the killers very likely came from a dissident clan in Hebron that has long been a thorn in the side of Hamas. Eldar added, "I'm sure they didn't get any green light from the leadership of Hamas, they just thought it was the right time to act."

The eighteen-day rampage after the kidnapping, however, succeeded in undermining the feared unity government, and sharply increasing Israeli repression. According to Israeli military sources, Israeli soldiers arrested 419 Palestinians, including 335 affiliated with Hamas, and killed six Palestinians, also searching thousands of locations and confiscating $350,000. Israel also conducted dozens of attacks in Gaza, killing five Hamas members on July 7.

Hamas finally reacted with its first rockets in nineteen months, providing Israel with the pretext for Operation Protective Edge on July 8.

By July 31, around 1,400 Palestinians had been killed, mostly civilians, including hundreds of women and children, and three Israeli civilians. By then, large areas of Gaza had been turned into rubble. During brief bombing pauses, relatives desperately sought shattered bodies or household items in the ruins of homes. Four hospitals had been attacked, each yet another war crime. The main power plant was attacked, sharply curtailing the already very limited electricity and worse still, reducing still further the minimal availability of fresh water. Another war crime. Meanwhile rescue teams and ambulances are repeatedly attacked. The atrocities mount throughout Gaza, while Israel claims that its goal is to destroy tunnels at the border.

Israeli officials laud the humanity of what it calls "the most moral army in the world," which informs residents that their homes will be bombed. The practice is "sadism, sanctimoniously disguising itself as mercy," in the words of Israeli journalist Amira Hass: "A recorded message demanding hundreds of thousands of people leave their already targeted homes, for another place, equally dangerous, 10 kilometers away."

In fact, there is no place in the prison of Gaza safe from Israeli sadism, which may even exceed the terrible crimes of Operation Cast Lead in 2008–2009.

The hideous revelations elicited the usual reaction from the most moral president in the world, Barack Obama: great sympathy for Israelis, bitter condemnation of Hamas, and calls for moderation on both sides.

When the current episode of sadism is called off, Israel hopes to be free to pursue its criminal policies in the Occupied Territories without interference, and with the US support it has enjoyed in the past: military, economic, and diplomatic; and also ideological, by framing the issues in conformity to Israeli doctrines. Gazans will be free to return to the norm in their Israeli-run prison, while in the West Bank Palestinians can watch in peace as Israel dismantles what remains of their possessions.

That is the likely outcome if the United States maintains its decisive and virtually unilateral support for Israeli crimes and its rejection of the long-standing international consensus on diplomatic settlement. But the future will be quite different if the United States withdraws that support.

In that case it would be possible to move toward the "enduring solution" in Gaza that US secretary of state John Kerry called for, eliciting hysterical condemnation in Israel because the phrase could be interpreted as calling for an end to Israel's siege and regular attacks. And—horror of horrors—the phrase might even be interpreted as calling for implementation of international law in the rest of the Occupied Territories.

It is not that Israel's security would be threatened by adherence to international law; it would very likely be enhanced. But as explained forty years ago by Israeli general Ezer Weizman, later president, Israel could then not "exist according to the scale, spirit, and quality she now embodies."

There are similar cases in recent history. Indonesian generals swore that they would never abandon what Australian foreign minister Gareth Evans called "the Indonesian Province of East Timor" as he was making a deal to steal Timorese oil. And as long as they retained US support through decades of virtually genocidal slaughter, their goals were realistic. In September 1999, under considerable domestic and international pressure, President Clinton finally informed them quietly that the game was over and they instantly withdrew—while Evans turned to his new career as the lauded apostle of "responsibility to protect," to be sure, in a version designed to permit Western resort to violence at will.

Another relevant case is South Africa. In 1958, South Africa's foreign minister informed the US ambassador that although his country was becoming a pariah state, it would not matter as long as the US support continued. His assessment proved fairly accurate. Thirty years later, Reagan was the last significant holdout in supporting the apartheid regime. Within a few years, Washington joined the world, and the regime collapsed—not for that reason alone of course; one crucial factor was the remarkable Cuban role in the liberation of Africa, generally ignored in the West though not in Africa.

Forty years ago Israel made the fateful decision to choose expansion over security, rejecting a full peace treaty offered by Egypt in return for evacuation from the occupied Egyptian Sinai, where Israel was initiating extensive settlement and development projects. It has adhered to that policy ever since, making essentially the same judgment as South Africa did in 1958.

In the case of Israel, if the United States decided to join the world, the impact would be far greater. Relations of power allow nothing else, as has been demonstrated over and over when Washington has demanded that Israel abandon cherished goals. Furthermore, Israel by now has little recourse, after having adopted policies that turned it from a country that was greatly admired to one that is feared and despised, policies it is pursuing with blind determination today in its resolute march toward moral deterioration and possible ultimate destruction.

Could US policy change? It's not impossible. Public opinion has shifted considerably in recent years, particularly among the young, and it cannot be completely ignored.

For some years there has been a good basis for public demands that Washington observe its own laws and cut off military aid to Israel. US law requires that "no security assistance may be provided to any country the government of which engages in a consistent pattern of gross violations of internationally recognized human rights." Israel most certainly is guilty of this consistent pattern, and has been for many years.

Senator Patrick Leahy of Vermont, author of this provision of the law, has brought up its potential applicability to Israel in specific cases, and with a well-conducted educational, organizational, and activist effort such initiatives could be pursued successfully.

That could have a very significant impact in itself, while also providing a springboard for further actions to compel Washington to become part of "the international community" and to observe international law and norms.

Nothing could be more significant for the tragic Palestinian victims of many years of violence and repression.

CHAPTER TEN

The Futility and Immorality of Partition in Palestine

Ilan Pappé

There is a famous Jewish maxim that one should look for one's lost key where it was lost and not where there is light. In many ways, the so-called peace process in Palestine, with the concept of the two-state solution as its benchmark, has been a futile search under a powerful streetlamp far away from the lost key.

The congregation of world leaders, mediators, liberal Zionists, so-called moderate Palestinians, and some of Palestine's best friends in the West under the street lamp was motivated by a shared misconception of the Palestine conflict as one fought between two national movements. From within this perspective two other misconceptions emerge: the conflict in Palestine started more or less in 1967 with the occupation by Israel of the West Bank and the Gaza Strip, and secondly, these two areas are more "Palestinian" in nature and history than the rest of Palestine. Away from the lamp lie truths which are uncomfortable it seems not only to Zionists but also to those who fear a direct confrontation with the Jewish state. There in the darkness one can find the only relevant framing of the conflict in Palestine: as a struggle between a settler-colonialist movement and a native indigenous population that has raged since the late nineteenth century until today.

Seen from the perspective of settler colonialism the conflict is a relentless and tireless engagement with the attempt to take over as much of Palestine as possible and leave in it as few Palestinians as possible. Ironically, the wish to de-Arabize the country stemmed from a Zionist aspiration to create a European kind of democracy within the midst of the Arab world with one caveat only: it had to be a Jewish democracy.

Hence the colonialist impulse of the settlers was always geographical and demographic. The movement in its early stages was led by pragmatic leaders, such as David Ben-Gurion, who recognized the need to take over Palestine bit by bit and without forgetting the imperative of always having an exclusive Jewish majority in the land. And therefore when the Jews were less than a third of the population during the mandatory period (1918–1948), the movement proposed a partition of Palestine in a way that would ensure the small minority of settlers' demographic exclusivity in parts of Palestine, with the hope of absorbing more settlers in the future and thus more land. In fact, early on—in the 1930s—the Zionist leaders tried to persuade the British government to help materialize these dreams by transferring Palestinians from future Jewish areas as part of a solution to the emerging conflict; but the empire was not convinced.

So the Zionist movement had to do it itself, namely had to contemplate both the takeover of the space for a future Jewish democracy and the removal of the Palestinians living in that space. The need to use force in order to change the demographic balance in a country in which the Jewish settlers were still only one-third in 1948 was accentuated by the failure of the Zionist movement to purchase a significant number of lands. The inevitable result was a vast ethnic cleansing operation in Palestine that had begun even before the British left the country in February 1948 and ended in early 1949.[1]

This ethnic cleansing operation created the West Bank and the Gaza Strip—two geopolitical entities that came to the world as part of the incremental takeover of Palestine by the Zionist movement (as did a third area, Wadi Ara, which was part of the West Bank but was annexed to Israel under duress, when Jordan was threatened with war and conceded this slice of the West Bank to Israel in April 1949 as part of the bilateral armistice agreement).[2]

The West Bank was carved out of the parts of Palestine allocated to an Arab state in the UN Partition resolution of November 29, 1947. It was the quid pro quo for a Jordanian consent to take only a limited part in the overall Arab attempt to salvage Palestine (the Jordanian Legion and the nascent Israeli army fought a bitter battle over Jerusalem and divided it between the two sides). The Gaza Strip was carved out of the Naqab or Negev and was created by Israel as a huge receptor of refugees. Israeli forces systematically cleansed all the villages and inhabitants south of Jaffa and pushed them into what became the Gaza Strip.[3] So these two geopolitical units were the leftovers of the Zionist attempt to Judaize the whole of Palestine—one was created as a result of a strategic understanding with Jordan; the other for the purpose of solving the demographic issue.

This was the real partition of Palestine until 1967. The fictive "peace partition," the streetlamp, was conceived by Israel after the 1967 war. It came within a set of strategic decisions taken by the thirteenth government of Israel. The background for these decisions was a discontent among many of Israel's chief policy makers about the 1948 tacit alliance with Jordan. There was an active lobby pushing Prime Minister Ben-Gurion, who was in power until 1963, to reconsider this alliance and find a pretext to occupy either parts of the West Bank or the whole of it. These were powerful people; some of them were generals in the 1948 war, such as Yigal Alon and Moshe Dayan, others were ideologues who considered the West Bank as the heart of ancient Israel without which the Jewish state could not survive. The military men also concocted the myth of the River Jordan as a natural barrier for future invasions from the east against the Jewish state. Anyone who had seen the River Jordan, even on a particular good day, would know that this creek could hardly stop a unit of donkeys, let alone tanks.[4]

This lobby had its chance to transform expansionist dreams into strategic planning once Ben-Gurion left office in 1963. Ben-Gurion was adamant in his objection for occupying any more parts of Palestine since he dreaded the incorporation of an additional and large number of Palestinians. But once he was gone, the government intensified its preparations for the eventuality of such an expansion. While Ben-Gurion was in charge he prevented a dangerous circumstance from developing into a war—circumstances quite similar to the ones which led to the 1967 war. In 1960, Gamal Abdul Nasser, the leader of Egypt and the Arab world, embarked on a brinkmanship policy that foreshadowed his moves in 1967. A different Israeli prime minister and a different UN secretary general did not prevent a war that their predecessors successfully diffused in 1960.[5]

From 1963 onward, Israeli strategists intensified their preparations for the eventuality of a future occupation of the West Bank and the Gaza Strip. These preparations included very systematic planning for how to run the two areas as occupied military zones.[6] They were put into effective use within a few days in June 1967. But they were not enough; a strategy had to be formulated and this task was taken up by the Israeli government in several meetings during the following months after the fighting subsided.

Immediately after the 1967 war ended the thirteenth government of Israel began discussions that produced a series of decisions that all in one way or another condemned all the people who lived in the West Bank and the Gaza Strip to life imprisonment in the biggest ever human mega-prison witnessed in modern times. The Palestinians living there were incarcerated in such a fashion for crimes they never committed and for offenses that were never ever pronounced, admitted, or defined. Today a third generation of such "inmates" have begun their life in that mega-prison.

The particular government which took this callous and inhuman decision represented the widest possible Zionist consensus: every ideological stream and view was presented in that government. Socialists from Mapam sat alongside the Revisionist Menachem Begin and shared the glory and the power with the various factions that made up the Zionist Labor movement. They were joined by members of the most secular liberal and the most religious and ultra-religious political parties. Never before, nor after, during this government's term in office, would such a consensual partnership lead the state of Israel in its future and crucial decisions.

Contrary to common wisdom about the history of the West Bank and the Gaza Strip, no one apart from the government of Israel played any crucial role, then and ever since, in deciding the fate of these territories or the people living in them. What these ministers decided in the second half of June 1967, and in the following months of July and August, has remained to this day the cornerstone of Israeli policy toward the Occupied Territories. None of the successive Israeli governments deviated from these past decisions, nor did they wish to deviate from them in any form or shape.

The resolutions taken in that short period of three months, between June and August 1967, charted clearly the principles to which future governments in Israel would religiously adhere and from which they would not diverge, even during the most dramatic events that followed in years to come, be it the first or second Intifada or the Oslo peace process and the Camp David summit of 2000.

One explanation for the resilience of this set of decisions is the extraordinary composition of the 1967 government. As mentioned this government represented, as never before and never since, the widest possible Zionist consensus. One can also attribute it to the euphoric mood in the wake of the total devastation of six Arab armies by the IDF and the successful blitzkrieg that ended with the military occupation of vast areas of Arab lands and countries. A messianic aura surrounded the decision makers in those days energizing them to take bold and historic decisions, which their successors would find hard to refute or change.

All these plausible explanations tend to see the policies as the direct product of the particular and extraordinary circumstances of

June 1967. But these decisions were mainly the inevitable outcome of Zionist ideology and history (however one chooses to define this ideology or insist on its shades and innuendoes). The particular circumstances made it easier to remind the politicians of their ideological heritage and reconnected them once more, as they did in 1948, to the Zionist drive to Judaize as much of historical Palestine as possible.

The first decision was not to ethnically cleanse the population despite the joy of expanding the Jewish state onto what many Israelis felt were the natural and historical borders of ancient Israel. The ministers played with the idea but eventually ruled it out. They doubted whether the army had the will and mentality to carry it out, as it was unclear whether the army had sufficient means for accomplishing it.[7]

The second decision was to exclude the West Bank and the Gaza Strip from any future deal based on territories for peace (a principle that, at least in theory, the government accepted for the Sinai Peninsula and the Golan Heights). The prevailing sense in those meetings was that the international immunity for land expansion was guaranteed—not as an endorsement of expansionism per se but more as an unwillingness to confront it. But with one crucial caveat: there could not be a de jure annexation of the territories, only a de facto one.[8]

The third one was not to grant full citizenship to the occupied population so as not to endanger the demographic Jewish majority. There was then, and there is now, a consensual Israeli impulse and overwhelming desire to keep the West Bank forever, while at the same time there was and is the twofold recognition of the undesirability of officially annexing these territories and the inability to expel the population en masse. The aspirations about the Gaza Strip then and now are more ambivalent—the main drive was to see it disappear. It was a vision in 1967 which has become a dangerous blueprint for action these days. And yet keeping these territories, with the population in it, seemed as vital as the need to maintain a decisive Jewish majority in whatever constituted a Jewish state.

The minutes of the meetings are now open to historians. They expose the impossibility and incompatibility of these two impulses: the appetite for possessing new land on the one hand and the reluctance to either drive out or fully incorporate the people living on them, on the other. But the documents also reveal a self-congratulatory satisfaction from the early discovery of a way out of the ostensible logical deadlock and theoretical impasse. The ministers were convinced, as all the ministers after them would be, that they had found the formula that would enable Israel to keep the territories it coveted, without annexing the people it negated and while safeguarding its international immunity and reputation.[9]

When those three goals are translated into actual policies they can only produce an inhuman and ruthless reality on the ground. There can be no benign or enlightened version for a policy meant to keep people in citizenless status for a long period of time. Only one known human invention operates in such a way which robs temporarily, or for longer period of times, the basic human and civil rights of citizens: the modern-day prison.

The official Israeli navigation between impossible nationalist and colonialist ambitions turned a million and half people in 1967 into inmates of such a mega-prison; it was not a prison for a few inmates wrongly or rightly incarcerated: it was imposed on a society as a whole. It was and still is a system of malice that was built due to vile motives, but not only. Some of its architects searched genuinely for the most possible humane model for this prison; probably because they were aware that this was a collective punishment for a crime never committed. Others did not even bother to search for a softer version or more humane one. But the two camps existed and therefore the government offered two versions of the mega-prison to the people in the West Bank and the Gaza Strip. One was an open-air prison and the other a maximum security one. Should they not accept the former, they would get the latter.

The open-air prison allowed a measure of autonomous life under indirect and direct Israeli control; the maximum security one robbed the Palestinians of all the autonomies and subjected them to a harsh policy of punishments, restriction, and in the worst-case scenario execution. The reality on the ground was that the open-air prison was harsh enough and sufficiently inhuman to trigger resistance from the enclaved population and that the maximum security model was imposed as retaliation to Palestinian resistance. In general the softer model was attempted twice between 1967 and 1987 and between 1993 and 2000, and the retaliations occurred in 1987 until 1993 and 2000 until 2009.

The open-air prison became the false paradigm of peace as it was marketed by Israel, and by American and European allies of the Jewish state, as an ingenious idea for how to solve the conflict. The best open prison was eventually propagated first as an autonomous zone, in the 1979 Camp David agreement between Israel and Egypt that led to nowhere, and later on as an independent Palestinian state in the Oslo Accord of 1993. When the Oslo accord was translated into reality, by the sheer power of the occupier, the resemblance of the idea of a "state" to an open prison became clear with the partitioning of the West Bank into Areas A, B, and C and the exclusion of the Jewish settlements in Gaza from any Palestinian rule. The map of the Oslo B accord of 1994 gave autonomy only in small parts of the West Bank and the Gaza Strip, but left the control of the enclaves' security and sovereignty in the hands of the Israeli security apparatuses. When the Israeli regime felt security deteriorated for a short while, the maximum security model was reinstalled in 2002 and in many ways it is still there today while the rebellious prison of Gaza is severely punished by a continuous siege and closure.

The success of turning the open-prison model into a diplomatic effort and a "peace process" could not have been possible had it not won the support of large sections of the Palestinian political elite, the Zionist Left, and even some very well-known and highly respected international supporters of the Palestinian cause. But it is mainly a new creation, the Quartet, a kind of ad hoc international tribunal for Palestine, consisting of the European Union, Russia, the United States, and the United Nations, that gave the process the legitimacy it needed to be seen as a powerful paradigm for peace.

In Israel and in the West, a huge laundry list of words and a very cooperative media and academia were essential for maintaining the moral and political validity of the open-air prison option as the best solution for the "conflict" and as an ideal vision for normal and healthy life in the occupied West Bank and the Gaza Strip. "Autonomy," "self-determination," and finally "independence" were used, and mainly abused, as words to describe the best version of an open-air prison model the Israelis could offer the Palestinians in the West Bank and the Gaza Strip.

But this laundry list did not cleanse the reality, and the hyperbolic discourse of peace and independence did not deafen the conscientious members of all the societies involved: in the territories, in Israel, and in the outside world. In the age of the Internet, an independent press, an active civil society, and energetic NGOs, it was hard to play the charade of peace and reconciliation on the ground where people were incarcerated in the biggest ever human prison witnessed in modern history.

In this situation, out of conscious intention to control the area indefinitely and deny all the human rights of its people, Israel invented the magic formula of presenting the occupation as temporary. The status of the population will be settled "with the coming of peace." This mode of operation allows Israel to continue to present itself as a "democratic state" and enjoy the many benefits attached to this status in the international arena.

Hence "the peace process" and talk about "two states for two peoples" are not in any contradiction with the occupation, not even the "temporary occupation" of 1967. They are a political and conceptual framework designed to enable and perpetuate the status quo for as long as possible.

Israel would find it hard to market this façade to the world if it were not assisted by many others, some serving their self-interests and others out of misled good intentions. The leadership of the Palestinian national movement also plays a key role in providing credibility for the fake peace process. It is followed by a large part of the leadership of the Palestinian Arab population within the Green Line. Many peace activists around the world have fallen into this trap.

Meanwhile, Israel has been working on the ground to deepen

its control over the land, water, economy, and all aspects of Palestinian lives. It creates a situation where even if a Palestinian state is announced, headed by Mahmoud Abbas as president, it will not have any practical significance.

There is no chance of getting out of the deadlock in Palestine without tearing apart the façade of a fake peace process and the two-state solution. It is time to look for the key where we lost it. We need to start by correctly identifying the problem: expose Zionism as a colonialist movement and characterize Israel as an apartheid racist state. There is no other Zionism nor other Israel. Exposure, by itself, may have a huge effect: because of the importance of international support in preserving Israel's superiority against all local forces, but also due to internal conflicts within Israeli society.

Any solution should be derived from our understanding of the problem. It should start with a discussion among all residents of the country on how to live together within a framework where all enjoy full rights, equality, and partnership. The Palestinian refugees should also take part in this discussion, as they have the right to return to Palestine and to fully take part in shaping their country's future. It is essential to set the goal of establishing one state for all inhabitants and refugees of the country, because it defines who should participate in the discussion about this future.

Zionism has done, and continues to do, whatever it can to divide the Palestinian people and guide all of them to a dead end. First came the distancing of the refugees outside Palestine's borders and the isolation of the Palestinian population in the 1948 territories. Today we also witness the political separation between the West Bank and the Gaza Strip. Posing a new agenda, common to all sectors of the Palestinian people, is the beginning of the road toward a solution. Today's technology can provide the basis for an open discussion across borders and checkpoints, forming a platform for more intense links and together designing the common path.

All this is not at all easy. There are problems in the relationship between different sectors of the public, between secular and religious folk, between the indigenous inhabitants and the third generation of settlers. A new distribution of resources is required to compensate for generations of dispossession and discrimination. It is not clear what will be the nature of the new society and what political framework we will build together; but it is essential that we start a serious discussion about all of it. Beyond that we face a hard struggle against an oppressive regime that regards any perspective other than that of a racist Jewish state as "suicide" and an "existential danger."

This is our task and those are the problems we must solve. Until we look straight at this reality, we are wasting precious time. Understanding the problem and presenting a real solution can create strong dynamics for changing the balance of power.

CHAPTER ELEVEN

Ceasefires in Which Violations Never Cease

Noam Chomsky

On August 26, 2014, Israel and the Palestinian Authority (PA) both accepted a ceasefire agreement after a fifty-day Israeli assault on Gaza that left 2,100 Palestinians dead and vast landscapes of destruction behind. The agreement calls for an end to military action by both Israel and Hamas, as well as an easing of the Israeli siege that has strangled Gaza for many years.

This is, however, just the most recent of a series of ceasefire agreements reached after each of Israel's periodic escalations of its unremitting assault on Gaza. Throughout this period, the terms of these agreements remain essentially the same. The regular pattern is for Israel, then, to disregard whatever agreement is in place, while Hamas observes it—as Israel has officially recognized—until a sharp increase in Israeli violence elicits a Hamas response, followed

---

Adapted from "Ceasefires in Which Violations Never Cease," *TomDispatch*, September 9, 2014.

by even fiercer brutality. Rather than "mowing the lawn," in Israeli parlance, the most recent was more accurately described as "removing the topsoil" by a senior US military officer, appalled by the practices of the self-described "most moral army in the world."

The first of this series was the Agreement on Movement and Access Between Israel and the PA in November 2005. It called for a crossing between Gaza and Egypt at Rafah for the export of goods and the transit of people, continuous operation of crossings between Israel and Gaza for the import/export of goods, and the transit of people, reduction of obstacles to movement within the West Bank, bus and truck convoys between the West Bank and Gaza, the building of a seaport in Gaza, and the reopening of the airport in Gaza that Israeli bombing had demolished.

That agreement was reached shortly after Israel withdrew its settlers and military forces from Gaza. The motive for the disengagement was explained by Dov Weissglass, a confidant of then prime minister Ariel Sharon, who was in charge of negotiating and implementing it. "The significance of the disengagement plan is the freezing of the peace process," Weissglass informed the Israeli press. "And when you freeze that process, you prevent the establishment of a Palestinian state, and you prevent a discussion on the refugees, the borders, and Jerusalem. Effectively, this whole package called the Palestinian state, with all that it entails, has been removed indefinitely from our agenda. And all this with authority and permission. All with a [US] presidential blessing and the ratification of both houses of Congress." True enough.

"The disengagement is actually formaldehyde," Weissglass added. "It supplies the amount of formaldehyde that is necessary so there will not be a political process with the Palestinians." Israeli hawks also recognized that instead of investing substantial resources in maintaining a few thousand settlers in illegal communities in devastated Gaza, it made more sense to transfer them to illegal subsidized communities in areas of the West Bank that Israel intended to keep.

The disengagement was depicted as a noble effort to pursue peace, but the reality was quite different. Israel never relinquished control of Gaza and is, accordingly, recognized as the occupying power by the United Nations, the United States, and other states (Israel apart, of course). In their comprehensive history of Israeli settlement in the Occupied Territories, Israeli scholars Idith Zertal and Akiva Eldar describe what actually happened when that country disengaged: the ruined territory was not released "for even a single day from Israel's military grip or from the price of the occupation that the inhabitants pay every day." After the disengagement, "Israel left behind scorched earth, devastated services, and people with neither a present nor a future. The settlements were destroyed in an ungenerous move by an unenlightened occupier, which in fact continues to control the territory and kill and harass its inhabitants by means of its formidable military might."

Operations Cast Lead and Pillar of Defense

Israel soon had a pretext for violating the November agreement more severely. In January 2006, the Palestinians committed a serious crime. They voted "the wrong way" in carefully monitored free elections, placing the Parliament in the hands of Hamas. Israel and the United States immediately imposed harsh sanctions,

telling the world very clearly what they mean by "democracy promotion." Europe, to its shame, went along as well.

The United States and Israel soon began planning a military
coup to overthrow the unacceptable elected government, a familiar procedure. When Hamas preempted the coup in 2007, the
siege of Gaza became far more severe, along with regular Israeli
military attacks. Voting the wrong way in a free election was bad
enough, but preempting a US-planned military coup proved to be
an unpardonable offense.

A new ceasefire agreement was reached in June 2008. It again
called for opening the border crossings to "allow the transfer of all
goods that were banned and restricted to go into Gaza." Israel formally agreed to this, but immediately announced that it would not
abide by the agreement and open the borders until Hamas released
Gilad Shalit, an Israeli soldier held by Hamas.

Israel itself has a long history of kidnapping civilians in
Lebanon and on the high seas and holding them for lengthy peri-
ods without credible charge, sometimes as hostages. Of course,
imprisoning civilians on dubious charges, or none, is a regular
practice in the territories Israel controls. But the standard Western distinction between people and "unpeople" (in Orwell's useful
phrase) renders all this insignificant.

Israel not only maintained the siege in violation of the June
2008 ceasefire agreement but did so with extreme rigor, even preventing the United Nations Relief and Works Agency, which
cares for the huge number of official refugees in Gaza, from re-
plenishing its stocks.

On November 4, while the media were focused on the US presidential election, Israeli troops entered Gaza and killed half a dozen

Hamas militants. That elicited a Hamas missile response and an exchange of fire. (All the deaths were Palestinian.) In late December, Hamas offered to renew the ceasefire. Israel considered the offer, but rejected it, preferring instead to launch Operation Cast Lead, a three-week incursion of the full power of the Israeli military into the Gaza Strip, resulting in shocking atrocities well documented by international and Israeli human rights organizations.

On January 8, 2009, while Cast Lead was in full fury, the UN Security Council passed a unanimous resolution (with the United States abstaining) calling for "an immediate ceasefire leading to a full Israeli withdrawal, unimpeded provision through Gaza of food, fuel, and medical treatment, and intensified international arrangements to prevent arms and ammunition smuggling."

A new ceasefire agreement was indeed reached, but the terms, similar to the previous ones, were again never observed and broke down completely with the next major mowing-the-lawn episode in November 2012, Operation Pillar of Defense. What happened in the interim can be illustrated by the casualty figures from January 2012 to the launching of that operation: one Israeli was killed by fire from Gaza while seventy-eight Palestinians were killed by Israeli fire.

The first act of Operation Pillar of Defense was the murder of Ahmed Jabari, a high official of the military wing of Hamas. Aluf Benn, editor in chief of Israel's leading newspaper *Haaretz*, described Jabari as Israel's "subcontractor" in Gaza, who enforced relative quiet there for more than five years. As always, there was a pretext for the assassination, but the likely reason was provided by Israeli peace activist Gershon Baskin. He had been involved in direct negotiations with Jabari for years and reported that, hours before he was assassinated, Jabari "received the draft of a permanent truce agreement with Israel, which included mechanisms for maintaining the ceasefire in the case of a flare-up between Israel and the factions in the Gaza Strip."

There is a long record of Israeli actions designed to deter the threat of a diplomatic settlement. After this exercise of mowing the lawn, a ceasefire agreement was reached yet again. Repeating the now-standard terms, it called for a cessation of military action by both sides and the effective ending of the siege of Gaza with Israel, "opening the crossings and facilitating the movements of people and transfer of goods, and refraining from restricting residents' free movements and targeting residents in border areas."

What happened next was reviewed by Nathan Thrall, senior Middle East analyst of the International Crisis Group. Israeli intelligence recognized that Hamas was observing the terms of the ceasefire. "Israel," Thrall wrote, "therefore saw little incentive in upholding its end of the deal. In the three months following the ceasefire, its forces made regular incursions into Gaza, strafed Palestinian farmers and those collecting scrap and rubble across the border, and fired at boats, preventing fishermen from accessing the majority of Gaza's waters." In other words, the siege never ended. "Crossings were repeatedly shut. So-called buffer zones inside Gaza [from which Palestinians are barred, and which include a third or more of the strip's limited arable land] were reinstated. Imports declined, exports were blocked, and fewer Gazans were given exit permits to Israel and the West Bank."

Operation Protective Edge

So matters continued until April 2014, when an important event took place. The two major Palestinian groupings, Gaza-based Hamas and the Fatah-dominated PA in the West Bank, signed a unity agreement. Hamas made major concessions. The unity government contained none of its members or allies. In substantial measure, as Nathan Thrall observes, Hamas turned over governance of Gaza to the PA. Several thousand PA security forces were sent there and the PA placed its guards at borders and crossings, with no reciprocal positions for Hamas in the West Bank security apparatus. Finally, the unity government accepted the three conditions that Washington and the European Union had long demanded: nonviolence, adherence to past agreements, and the recognition of Israel.

Israel was infuriated. Its government declared at once that it would refuse to deal with the unity government and cancelled negotiations. Its fury mounted when the United States, along with most of the world, signaled support for the unity government.

There are good reasons why Israel opposes the unification of Palestinians. One is that the Hamas-Fatah conflict has provided a useful pretext for refusing to engage in serious negotiations. How can one negotiate with a divided entity? More significantly, for more than twenty years, Israel has been committed to separating Gaza from the West Bank in violation of the Oslo Accords it signed in 1993, which declare Gaza and the West Bank to be an inseparable territorial unity.

A look at a map explains the rationale. Separated from Gaza, any West Bank enclaves left to Palestinians have no access to the outside world. They are contained by two hostile powers, Israel and Jordan, both close US allies—and contrary to illusions, the United States is very far from a neutral "honest broker."

Furthermore, Israel has been systematically taking over the Jordan Valley, driving out Palestinians, establishing settlements, sinking wells, and otherwise ensuring that the region—about one-third of the West Bank, with much of its arable land—will ultimately be integrated into Israel along with the other regions that country is taking over. Hence remaining Palestinian cantons will be completely imprisoned. Unification with Gaza would interfere with these plans, which trace back to the early days of the occupation and have had steady support from the major political blocs, including figures usually portrayed as doves like former president Shimon Peres, who was one of the architects of settlement deep in the West Bank.

As usual, a pretext was needed to move on to the next escalation, which arose when three Israeli boys from the settler community in the West Bank were brutally murdered. The Israeli police have since been searching for and arresting members of a dissident group in Hebron, still claiming, without evidence, that they are "Hamas terrorists." On September 2, *Haaretz* reported that, after very intensive interrogations, the Israeli security services concluded the abduction of the teenagers "was carried out by an independent cell" with no known direct links to Hamas.

But the eighteen-day rampage by the Israeli Defense Forces succeeded in undermining the feared unity government and provoking Hamas to respond by firing its first rockets in eighteen months, providing Israel with the pretext to launch Operation Protective Edge on July 8. The fifty-day assault proved the most extreme exercise in mowing the lawn—so far.

Operation (Still to Be Named)

Israel is in a fine position today to reverse its decades-old policy of separating Gaza from the West Bank in violation of its solemn agreements and to observe a major ceasefire agreement for the first time. At least temporarily, the threat of democracy in neighboring Egypt has been diminished, and the brutal Egyptian military dictatorship of General Abdul Fattah al-Sisi is a welcome ally for Israel in maintaining control over Gaza.

The Palestinian unity government, as noted earlier, is placing the US-trained forces of the Palestinian Authority in control of Gaza's borders, and governance may be shifting into the hands of the PA, which depends on Israel for its survival, as well as for its finances. Israel might feel that its takeover of Palestinian territory in the West Bank has proceeded so far that there is little to fear from some limited form of autonomy for Palestinians in the enclaves that remain.

There is also some truth to Prime Minister Benjamin Netanyahu's observation: "Many elements in the region understand today that, in the struggle in which they are threatened, Israel is not an enemy but a partner." Akiva Eldar, Israel's leading diplomatic correspondent, adds, however, that "all those 'many elements in the region' also understand that there is no brave and comprehensive diplomatic move on the horizon without an agreement on the establishment of a Palestinian state based on the 1967 borders and a just, agreed-upon solution to the refugee problem." That is not on Israel's agenda, he points out, and is in fact in direct conflict with the 1999 electoral program of the governing Likud coalition, never rescinded, which "flatly rejects the establishment of a Palestinian Arab state west of the Jordan river."

Some knowledgeable Israeli commentators, notably columnist Danny Rubinstein, believe that Israel is poised to reverse course and relax its stranglehold on Gaza.

We'll see.

The record of these past years suggests otherwise and the first signs are not auspicious. As Operation Protective Edge ended, Israel announced its largest appropriation of West Bank land in thirty years, almost 1,000 acres. Israel Radio reported that the takeover was in response to the killing of the three Jewish teenagers by "Hamas militants." A Palestinian boy was burned to death in retaliation for the murder, but no Israeli land was handed to Palestinians, nor was there any reaction when an Israeli soldier murdered ten-year-old Khalil Anati on a quiet street in a refugee camp near Hebron on August 10, while the most moral army in the world was smashing Gaza to bits, and then drove away in his jeep as the child bled to death.

Anati was one of the twenty-three Palestinians (including three children) killed by Israeli occupation forces in the West Bank during the Gaza onslaught, according to UN statistics, along with more than two thousand wounded, 38 percent by live fire. "None of those killed were endangering soldiers' lives," Israeli journalist Gideon Levy reported. To none of this is there any reaction, just as there was no reaction while Israel killed, on average, more than two Palestinian children a week for the past fourteen years. They are *unpeople*, after all.

It is commonly claimed on all sides that, if the two-state settlement is dead as a result of Israel's takeover of Palestinian lands, then the outcome will be one state west of the Jordan. Some Palestinians welcome this outcome, anticipating that they can then conduct a civil rights struggle for equal rights on the model of South Africa under apartheid. Many Israeli commentators warn that the resulting "demographic problem" of more Arab than Jewish births and diminishing Jewish immigration will undermine their hope for a "democratic Jewish state."

But these widespread beliefs are dubious.

The realistic alternative to a two-state settlement is that Israel will continue to carry forward the plans it has been implementing for years, taking over whatever is of value to it in the West Bank, while avoiding Palestinian population concentrations and removing Palestinians from the areas it is integrating into Israel. That should avoid the dreaded "demographic problem."

The areas being integrated into Israel include a vastly expanded Greater Jerusalem, the area within the illegal "Separation Wall," and corridors cutting through the regions to the east, and will probably also encompass the Jordan Valley. Gaza will likely remain under its usual harsh siege, separated from the West Bank. And the Syrian Golan Heights—like Jerusalem, annexed in violation of Security Council orders—will quietly become part of Greater Israel. In the meantime, West Bank Palestinians will be contained in unviable cantons, with special accommodation for elites in standard neocolonial style.

These basic policies have been under way since the 1967 conquest, following a principle enunciated by then defense minister Moshe Dayan, one of the Israeli leaders most sympathetic to the Palestinians. He informed his party colleagues that they should tell Palestinian refugees in the West Bank, "We have no solution, you shall continue to live like dogs, and whoever wishes may leave, and we will see where this process leads."

The suggestion was natural within the overriding conception articulated in 1972 by future president Haim Herzog: "I do not deny the Palestinians a place or stand or opinion on every matter. . . . But certainly I am not prepared to consider them as partners in any respect in a land that has been consecrated in the hands of our nation for thousands of years. For the Jews of this land there cannot be any partner." Dayan also called for Israel's "permanent rule" ("*memshelet keva*") over the Occupied Territories. When Netanyahu expresses the same stand today, he is not breaking new ground.

Like other states, Israel pleads "security" as justification for its aggressive and violent actions. But knowledgeable Israelis know better. Their recognition of reality was articulated clearly in 1972 by air force commander (and later president) Ezer Weizman. He explained that there would be no security problem if Israel were to accept the international call to withdraw from the territories it conquered in 1967, but the country would not then be able to "exist according to the scale, spirit, and quality she now embodies."

For a century, the Zionist colonization of Palestine has proceeded primarily on the pragmatic principle of the quiet establishment of facts on the ground, which the world was to ultimately come to accept. It has been a highly successful policy. There is every reason to expect it to persist as long as the United States provides the necessary military, economic, diplomatic, and ideological support. For those concerned with the rights of the brutalized Palestinians, there can be no higher priority than working to change US policies, not an idle dream by any means.

CHAPTER TWELVE

An Address to the United Nations

Noam Chomsky

It's a pleasure to be here to be able to talk with you and discuss with you afterwards. Many of the world's problems are so intractable that it's hard to think of ways even to take steps toward mitigating them.

The Israel-Palestine conflict is not one of these.

On the contrary, the general outlines of a diplomatic solution have been clear for at least forty years. Not the end of the road—nothing ever is—but a significant step forward. And the obstacles to a resolution are also quite clear. The basic outlines were presented here in a resolution brought to the UN Security Council in January 1976. It called for a two-state settlement on the internationally recognized border—and now I'm quoting—"with guarantees for the rights of both states to exist in peace and security within secure and recognized borders." The resolution was

---

This essay is based on a speech delivered to the United Nations General Assembly on October 14, 2014.

brought by the three major Arab states: Egypt, Jordan, Syria—sometimes called the "confrontation states."

Israel refused to attend the session. The resolution was vetoed by the United States. A US veto typically is a double veto: the veto, the resolution, is not implemented, and the event is vetoed from history, so you have to look hard to find the record, but it is there. That has set the pattern that has continued since. The most recent US veto was in February 2011—that's President Obama—when his administration vetoed a resolution calling for implementation of official US policy opposition to expansion of settlements. And it's worth bearing in mind that expansion of settlements is not really the issue; it's the settlements, unquestionably illegal, along with the infrastructure projects supporting them. For a long time, there has been an overwhelming international consensus in support of a settlement along these general lines. The pattern that was set in January 1976 continues to the present. Israel rejects a settlement of these terms and for many years has been devoting extensive resources to ensuring that it will not be implemented, with the unremitting and decisive support of the United States—military, economic, diplomatic, and indeed ideological—by establishing how the conflict is viewed and interpreted in the United States and within its broad sphere of influence.

There's no time here to review the record, but its general character is revealed by a look at what has happened in Gaza in the past decade, carrying forward a long history of earlier crimes. Last August, August 26th, a ceasefire was reached between Israel and the Palestinian Authority. And the question on all our minds is: what are the prospects for the future? Well, one reasonable way to try to answer that question is to look at the record. And here, too, there is a definite pattern: A ceasefire is reached; Israel disregards it and continues its steady assault on Gaza, including continued siege, intermittent acts of violence, more settlement and development projects, often violence in the West Bank; Hamas observes the ceasefire, as Israel officially recognizes, until some Israeli escalation elicits a Hamas response, which leads to another exercise of "mowing the lawn," in Israeli parlance, each episode more fierce and destructive than the last. The first of the series was the Agreement on Movement and Access in November 2005. I'll give a close paraphrase of it. It called for a crossing between Gaza and Egypt at Rafah for the export of goods and the transit of people, continuous operation of crossings between Israel and Gaza for the import and export of goods and the transit of people, reduction of obstacles to movement within the West Bank, bus and truck convoys between the West Bank and Gaza, the building of a seaport in Gaza, the reopening of the airport in Gaza that Israel had recently destroyed. These are essentially the terms of successive ceasefires, including the one just reached a few weeks ago.

The timing of the November 2005 agreement is significant. This was the moment of Israel's disengagement, as it's called, from Gaza—the removal of several thousand Israeli settlers from Gaza. Now, this is depicted as a noble effort to seek peace and development, but the reality is rather different. The reality was described, very quickly, by the Israeli official who was in charge of negotiating and implementing the ceasefire, Dov Weissglass, close confidant of then prime minister Ariel Sharon. As he explained to the Israeli press, the goal of the disengagement—I'm quoting him—was "the freezing of the peace process," so as to "prevent the establishment of a Palestinian state" and to ensure that diplomacy "has been removed indefinitely from our agenda." The reality on the ground is described by Israel's leading specialists on the occupation—a respected historian, Idith Zertal, and Israel's leading diplomatic correspondent, Akiva Eldar, wrote the major book, the standard work on the settlement project, called *Lords of the Land*, referring to the settlers. What they say about the disengagement is this: They say, "the ruined territory"—and by then, it was ruined, largely part of the reason for the removal of the settlers—"the ruined territory was not released for even a single day from Israel's military grip, or from the price of the occupation that the inhabitants pay every day. After the disengagement, Israel left behind scorched earth, devastated services, and people with neither a present nor a future. The settlements were destroyed in an ungenerous move by an unenlightened occupier, which in fact continues to control the territory and to kill and harass its inhabitants by means of its formidable military might." Now, that's an accurate description from the most respected Israeli source.

The Oslo Accords, twenty years ago, established that Gaza and the West Bank are an indivisible territorial unity, whose integrity cannot be broken up. For twenty years, the United States and Israel have been dedicated to separate Gaza and the West Bank in violation of the accords that they had accepted. And a look at the map explains why. Gaza offers the only access to the outside world of Palestine. If Gaza is separated from the West Bank, whatever autonomy might ultimately be granted in the West Bank would be imprisoned—Israel on one side, a hostile Jordan, ally of Israel, on the other side, and in addition, one of Israel's slow and steady US-backed policies is to take over the Jordan Valley, about a third of the West Bank, much of the arable land, which would essentially imprison the rest even more tightly, if Gaza is separated from the West Bank. Now, that's the major geostrategic reason for the Israeli insistence, with US backing, on separating the two in violation of the Oslo agreements and the series of ceasefires that have been reached since November 2005.

Well, the November 2005 agreement lasted for a few weeks. In January 2006, a very important event took place: the first full, free election in the Arab world, carefully monitored, recognized to be free and fair. It had one flaw: it came out the wrong way. Hamas won the Parliament, control of the Parliament. The US and Israel didn't want that. You may recall, at that period, the slogan on everyone's lips was "democracy promotion." The highest US commitment in the world was democracy promotion. Here was a good test. Democracy: election came out the wrong way; the US instantly decided, along with Israel, to punish the Palestinians for the crime of voting the wrong way; a harsh siege was instituted, other punishments; violence increased; the United States immediately began to organize a military coup to overthrow the unacceptable government. That's quite familiar practice—I won't go through the record. The European Union, to its shame and discredit, went along with this. There was an immediate Israeli escalation. That was the end of the November agreement, followed by major Israeli onslaughts.

In 2007, a year later, Hamas committed even a greater crime than winning a fair election: it preempted the planned military coup and took over Gaza. That's described in the West, in the United States, most of the West, as Hamas's taking over Gaza by force—which is not false, but something is omitted. The force was preempting a planned military coup to overthrow the elected government. Now, that was a serious crime. It's bad enough to vote the wrong way in a free election, but to preempt a US-planned military coup is far more serious. The attack on Gaza increased substantially at that point, major Israeli onslaughts. Finally, in January 2008, another ceasefire was reached. Terms were pretty much the same as those that I quoted. Israel publicly rejected the ceasefire, said that it would not abide by it. Hamas observed the ceasefire, as Israel officially recognizes, despite Israel's refusal to do so.

Now, that continued until November 4, 2008. On November 4, which was the day of the US election, Israeli forces invaded Gaza, killed half a dozen Hamas militants. That led to Qassam rockets attacking Israel, [then a] huge Israeli response, lots of killings—all Palestinians, as usual. By the end of December, a couple of weeks later, Hamas offered to renew the ceasefire. The Israeli cabinet considered it and rejected it. This was a dovish cabinet, led by Ehud Olmert—rejected it and decided to launch the next major military operation. That was Cast Lead, which was a horrible operation, so much so that it caused a very substantial international reaction, investigations by a United Nations commission, Amnesty International, Human Rights Watch. In the middle of the assault—the assault, incidentally, was carefully timed to end immediately before President Obama's inauguration. He had already been elected, but he wasn't inaugurated yet, so when he was asked to comment on the ongoing atrocities, he responded by saying that he couldn't do so, the United States has only one president, and he wasn't president yet. He was talking about lots of other things, but not this. The attack was timed to end immediately before the inauguration, so he therefore could respond to the questions by saying, "Well, now is not the time to look at the past, let's look forward to the future."

Diplomats know very well that that's a standard slogan for those who are engaged in serious crime: "Let's forget about the past, let's look forward to a glorious future." Well, that was right in the middle of the assault. The Security Council did pass a resolution—unanimously, the US abstaining—calling for an immediate ceasefire with the usual terms. That was January 8, 2009. It was never observed, and it broke down completely with the next major episode of "mowing the lawn" in November 2012. Now, you can get a good sense of what was going on by looking at the casualty figures for the year 2012. Seventy-nine people were killed, seventy-eight of them Palestinians—the usual story. . . . As [leading Middle East analyst Nathan Thrall] writes, Israel recognized that Hamas was observing the terms of the ceasefire, and "therefore saw little incentive" in doing the same.

The military attacks on Gaza increased, along with more stringent restrictions on imports. Exports were blocked. Exit permits were blocked. That continued until April 2014, when Palestinians committed another crime: Gaza-based Hamas and West Bank–based Palestinian Authority signed a unity agreement. Israel was infuriated—infuriated even more when the world mostly supported it. Even the United States gave weak, but actual, support. Several reasons for the Israeli reaction. One is that unity between Gaza and the West Bank, between the two movements, would threaten the long-standing policies of separating the two, for the reasons that I mentioned. Another reason was that a unity government undermines one of the pretexts for Israel's refusal to participate in negotiations seriously—namely, how can we negotiate with an entity that is internally divided? Well, if they're unified, that pretext disappears.

Israel was infuriated. It launched major assaults on the Palestinians in the West Bank, primarily targeting Hamas. Hundreds
of people arrested, mostly Hamas members. Also Gaza, also
killings. There was a pretext, of course. There always is. The pretext was that three teenagers, Israeli teenagers, in the settlements
had been brutally murdered—captured and murdered. Israel
claimed officially that they thought that they were alive, so therefore launched a long, several weeks' assault on the West Bank, al-
leging that they were trying to find them alive. Meanwhile, the
arrests, attacks, and so on. It turns out that they knew immediately
that they had been killed. Now, they also knew immediately that it
was very unlikely that Hamas was involved. The government said
they had certain knowledge that Hamas had done it, but their own
leading specialists [like Shlomi Eldar] had pointed out right away
that the assault—which was a brutal crime—was very likely committed by members of a breakaway clan, the Qawasmeh clan in
Hebron, which was not given a green light by Hamas and had
been a thorn in [its] side. And that, apparently, is true, if you look
at the later arrests and punishments.

Anyway, that was a pretext for this assault, killings in Gaza,
too. That finally elicited a Hamas response. Then came Operation
Protective Edge, the one which was just completed, and more
brutal and destructive even than the ones that preceded it. The
pattern is very clear. And so far, at least, it appears to be continuing. The latest ceasefire was reached on August 26. It was followed at once by Israel's greatest land grab in thirty years, almost a
thousand acres in the Gush Etzion area near what's called
Jerusalem, Greater Jerusalem, about five times the size of anything
that Jerusalem ever was, taken over by Israel, annexed in violation

of Security Council orders. The US State Department informed the Israeli Embassy that—I'm quoting it now—"Israeli activity in Gush Etzion undermines American efforts to protect Israel at the United Nations," and urged that Israel shouldn't provide ammunition for "those at the [United Nations] who would interpret [Israel's] position as hardening."

Actually, that warning was given forty-seven years ago, in September 1967, at the time of Israel's first colonization, illegal colonization, of Gush Etzion. Israeli historian Gershom Gorenberg recently reminded us of this. Little has changed since, in the last forty-seven years, apart from the scale of the crimes, which continue, without a break, with constant US support. Well, as for the prospects, there is a conventional picture. It's repeated constantly on all sides—Israel, Palestine, independent commentators, diplomats. The picture that's presented is that there are two alternatives: either the two-state settlement, which represents an overwhelming international consensus, virtually everyone, and if that fails, there will have to be one state—Israel will take over the West Bank, the Palestinians will hand over the keys, as it's sometimes said. Palestinians often have favored that. They say then they will be able to carry out a civil rights struggle, maybe modeled on the anti-apartheid struggle in South Africa, fight for civil rights within the whole one state controlled by Israel. Now, Israelis criticize that on the grounds of what is called "the demographic problem," the fact that there will be too many non-Jews in a Jewish state—in fact, pretty soon a majority. Those are the alternatives that are presented, overwhelmingly, hardly an exception.

My own opinion, which I've written about repeatedly—without convincing many people, apparently, but I'll try to convince

you—is that this is a total illusion. Those are not the two alternatives. There are two alternatives, but they're different ones. One
alternative is the international consensus on a two-state settlement, basically the terms of January 1976. By now, it's virtually
everyone—the Arab League, the Organization of Islamic States,
[which] includes Iran, Europe, Latin America—informally, at
least, [just] about everyone. That's one option. The other option,
the realistic one, is that Israel will continue doing exactly what it is
doing right now, before our eyes, visible, with US support, which
is also visible. And what's happening is not a secret. You can open
the newspapers and read it. Israel is taking over what they call
Jerusalem, as I mentioned, a huge area, maybe five times the area
of historic Jerusalem, Greater Jerusalem, big area in the West
Bank, includes many Arab villages being dispossessed, destroyed,
bringing settlers in. All of this is doubly illegal. All the settlements
are illegal, as determined by the Security Council, advisory opinion of the International Court of Justice. But the Jerusalem settlements are doubly illegal, because they're also in violation of
explicit Security Council orders going back to 1968, with the US
actually voting for them at that time, barring any change in the
status of Jerusalem. But it continues. That's Greater Jerusalem.

There are then corridors extending to the east. One major corridor extending from Jerusalem almost to Jericho, virtually bisecting
the West Bank, includes the Israeli town of Maale Adumim,
which was built largely during the Clinton administration, with
the obvious purpose of bisecting the West Bank—still a little con-
tested territory, but that's the goal. There's another corridor further
to the north including the town of Ariel, partially bisecting what
remains. [And] another one further to the north including the

town of Kedumim. If you look at the map, these essentially break up the West Bank into pretty much cantons. It looks, from a map, as though a large territory is left, but that's misleading. Most of that is uninhabitable desert. And that's separate from what I mentioned before, the slow, steady takeover of the Jordan Valley to the east—again, about a third of the arable land, the country.

Israel has no official policy of taking it over, but they're pursuing the policy in the way that has been carried out now for a hundred years, literally—small steps so nobody notices, or at least people pretend not to notice, establish a military zone. The Palestinians who live there have to be displaced because it's a military zone, no settlement allowed, and pretty soon there's a military settlement, Nahal settlement, and another, then, sooner or later, it becomes an actual settlement. Meanwhile, dig wells, dispossess the population, set up green zones—a large variety of techniques which have, by now, reduced the Arab population from about 300,000 in 1967 to roughly 60,000 today. As I mentioned, that essentially imprisons what's left. I don't think Israel has any intention of taking over the Palestinian population concentrations, which are left out of this, these plans.

There are analogies often made to South Africa, but they're quite misleading. South Africa relied on its Black population. That was 85 percent of the population. It was its workforce. And they had to sustain them, just like slaveowners have to maintain their capital. They tried to sustain the population. They even tried to gain international support for the bantustans. Israel has no such attitude toward the Palestinians. They don't want to have anything to do with them. If they leave, that's fine. If they die, that's fine. In standard neocolonial pattern, Israel is establishing—permitting the establishment of a center for Palestinian elites in Ramallah, where you have nice restaurants and theaters and so on. Every Third World country under the colonial system had something like that. Now, that's the picture that's emerging. It's taking shape before our eyes. It has so far worked very well. If it continues, Israel will not face a demographic problem. When these regions are integrated slowly into Israel, actually, the proportion of Jews in Greater Israel will increase. There are very few Palestinians there. Those who are there are being dispossessed, kicked out. That's what's taking shape before our eyes. I think that's the realistic alternative to a two-state settlement. And there's every reason to expect it to continue as long as the United States supports it.

ACKNOWLEDGMENTS

I still have to pinch myself to believe that I am working on a second book with Noam Chomsky and Ilan Pappé.

Huge thanks to both of them for accepting and taking the time to do this again. It was amazing spending time with them in Cambridge, Massachusetts, at Noam's workplace, MIT, and hanging out with Ilan in Boston was priceless, too (even though he left at halftime during a Boston Celtics basketball game).

I love to be able to work with Haymarket Books, always. To do this again with Anthony Arnove was fantastic and Dao X. Tran did an amazing job as editor. Thanks to Laura Gottesdiener for helping organize and prepare the manuscript.

Huge thanks to the Lyonses for giving us such a great welcome in Boston! We loved staying and spending time with you.

My brother Florent was once again by my side throughout the process. He came to Boston with me and even took part in the "Brussels" interview with Ilan. He is crucial to everything I do.

My "families" (by blood or not) help me in ways they often do not even realize: Min, Dad, Mae, Christopher, Laury, Romane, Florence, Tania, Ewa, Maria, Fay, and Herve, Rafeef, Aneta, Noura, Kasia, William, Awatef, Aneta and Maximilien. Knowing that you exist makes me stronger.

Jeanne, you are my enabler. You are the one who makes things tick, the one who shows me the way and the right direction. You are my main source of energy, love, and laughs. You are my light. Everything I do has parts of you in it. The fact that we have, together, given life to two amazing boys, Leo and Thom, makes me much more hopeful about the present and the future and makes me appreciate the beauty of life in ways that did not exist before.

NOTES

Chapter Ten

1. Ilan Pappé, *The Ethnic Cleansing of Palestine* (Oxford: Oneworld, 2006).
2. On these negotiations see Avi Shlaim, *Collusion Across the Jordan: King Ab-dullah, the Zionist Movement, and the Partition of Palestine* (New York: Columbia University Press, 1988).
3. Pappé, *Ethnic Cleansing*, 193–99.
4. On this lobby see Tom Segev, *1967: Israel, the War, and the Year That Transformed the Middle East* (New York: Metropolitan Books, 2007).
5. Ami Gluska, *The Israeli Military and the Origins of the 1967 War* (London and New York: Routledge, 2007), 122–25.
6 On these plans see Ilan Pappé, "Revisiting 1967: The False Paradigm of Peace, Partition and Parity," *Settler Colonial Studies* 3, nos. 3–4 (2013): 341–51.
7. The minutes of these meeting are now open to the public in the Israel State Archives, Section 43.4, cabinet meeting of June 11–20, 1967.
8. Ibid. The crucial meetings were on June 18 and 19.
9. Ibid.

INDEX

"Passim" (literally "scattered") indicates intermittent discussion of a topic over a cluster of pages.

ABOUT HAYMARKET BOOKS

Haymarket Books is a radical, independent, nonprofit book publisher based in Chicago.

Our mission is to publish books that contribute to struggles for social and economic justice. We strive to make our books a vibrant and organic part of social movements and the education and development of a critical, engaged, international left. We take inspiration and courage from our namesakes, the Haymarket martyrs, who gave their lives fighting for a better world. Their 1886 struggle for the eight-hour day—which gave us May Day, the international workers' holiday—reminds workers around the world that ordinary people can organize and struggle for their own liberation. These struggles continue today across the globe—struggles against oppression, exploitation, poverty, and war.

Since our founding in 2001, Haymarket Books has published more than five hundred titles. Radically independent, we seek to drive a wedge into the risk-averse world of corporate book publishing. Our authors include Noam Chomsky, Arundhati Roy, Rebecca Solnit, Angela Y. Davis, Howard Zinn, Amy Goodman, Wallace Shawn, Mike Davis, Winona LaDuke, Ilan Pappé, Richard Wolff, Dave Zirin, Keeanga-Yamahtta Taylor, Nick Turse, Dahr Jamail, David Barsamian, Elizabeth Laird, Amira Hass, Mark Steel, Avi Lewis, Naomi Klein, and Neil Davidson. We are also the trade publishers of the acclaimed Historical Materialism Book Series and of Dispatch Books.

ABOUT THE CONTRIBUTORS

Noam Chomsky is Institute Professor in the Department of Linguistics and Philosophy at the Massachusetts Institute of Technology, Boston. He is widely regarded as one of the foremost critics of U.S. foreign policy in the world. His books include *At War with Asia*, *Towards a New Cold War*, *Fateful Triangle*, *Necessary Illusions*, *Hegemony or Survival*, *Deterring Democracy*, *Failed States*, and *Manufacturing Consent*.

Professor Ilan Pappé is the Director of the European Center for Palestine Studies and a fellow at the Institute of Arab and Islamic Studies at the University of Exeter. He is the author of fifteen books, among them *The Ethnic Cleansing of Palestine* and his most recent book, *The Idea of Israel: A History of Power and Knowledge*.

Frank Barat is a human rights activists and author. He was the coordinator of the Russell Tribunal on Palestine and is now the president of the Palestine Legal Action Network. His books include: *Gaza in Crisis* and *Corporate Complicity in Israel's Occupation*. He can be contacted @frankbarat22 on Twitter.